the
baby owner's
manual

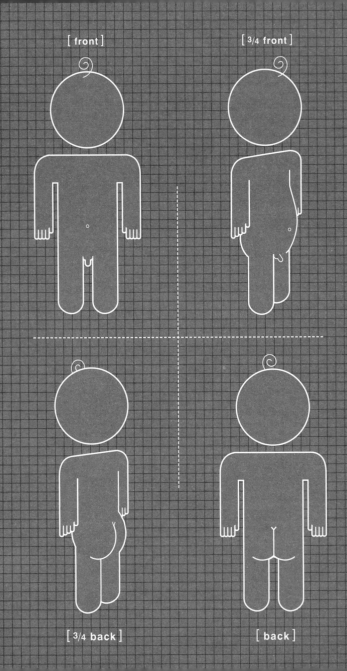

[front] [3/4 front]

[3/4 back] [back]

the baby

owner's manual

OPERATING INSTRUCTIONS, TROUBLE-SHOOTING
TIPS, AND ADVICE ON FIRST-YEAR MAINTENANCE

by Louis Borgenicht, M.D., and Joe Borgenicht, D.A.D.

Illustrated by Paul Kepple and Jude Buffum

QUIRK BOOKS
PHILADELPHIA

Library of Congress Cataloging in Publication Number: 2012900532

ISBN: 978-1-59474-597-3

Printed in China

Typeset in Swiss

Designed by Paul Kepple and Jude Buffum @ Headcase Design
Production management by John J. McGurk

Quirk Books
215 Church Street
Philadelphia, PA 19106
quirkbooks.com

10 9 8

Contents

CHAPTER 3:
FEEDING: UNDERSTANDING THE BABY'S POWER SUPPLY . . . 66

CHAPTER 6:
GROWTH AND DEVELOPMENT 156

Welcome
to Your New Baby!

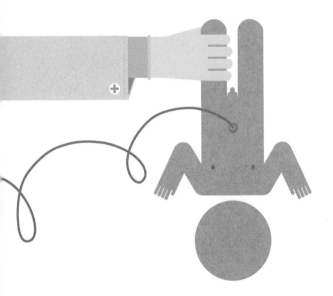

Congratulations on the arrival of your new baby.

This baby is surprisingly similar to other appliances you may already own. Like a personal computer, for instance, the baby will require a source of power to execute her many complicated tasks and functions. Like an inkjet printer, the baby's head will require frequent cleanings for optimum performance. And like an automobile, the baby may expel unpleasant odors into the atmosphere.

But there is one major difference: personal computers, inkjet printers, and automobiles all come with instruction manuals. Newborn babies do not—hence the book you are holding in your hands. *The Baby Owner's Manual* is a comprehensive user's guide to deriving maximum performance and optimal results from your newborn.

It is not necessary to read this entire manual cover to cover. For ease of use, this guide has been divided into seven separate sections. If you have a question or encounter a problem, just turn to any of the following chapters:

PREPARATION AND HOME INSTALLATION (pages 20–37) describes the best ways to anticipate the arrival of the baby. It features useful information on the configuration of the baby's nursery and the selection of transportation accessories (including popular devices known as *strollers* and *carriers*).

GENERAL CARE (pages 38–65) features effective techniques for handling, holding, and comforting the baby. It also illustrates complex procedures such as *swaddling* and *baby massage*, and presents toy accessories that may enhance the baby's intelligence.

FEEDING (pages 66–105) offers an in-depth guide to understanding the baby's power supply. This chapter includes detailed instructions on breastfeeding, bottle-feeding, burping the baby, and the introduction of solid food.

PROGRAMMING SLEEP MODE (pages 106–125) describes proven techniques for teaching the baby to sleep through the night. It also includes instructions on sleep malfunction, dealing with overstimulation, and configuring the baby's sleeping area.

GENERAL MAINTENANCE (pages 126–155) is important for the safety, sanitation, and well-being of all newborn models. This chapter features detailed instructions on re-installing diapers, cleaning the baby, and shortening the baby's hair.

GROWTH AND DEVELOPMENT (pages 156–179) teaches the user how to test baby reflexes and identify important milestones. This chapter also explains advanced motor and sensory applications, such as *crawling*, *pulling up*, and *baby talk*.

SAFETY AND EMERGENCY MAINTENANCE (pages 180–217) explores the best ways to childproof the baby's environment. It also features extremely important advice on the Heimlich maneuver and cardiopulmonary resuscitation, and monitoring the baby's health. Users can also refer to an A-to-Z guide of minor medical conditions like *cradle cap*, *hiccups*, and *pink eye*.

When used properly, the baby will provide years of love, devotion, and joy. But understanding how to use the baby takes practice, so it is important to be patient. Over the next few months, you may experience feelings of frustration, incompetence, hopelessness, and despair. These feelings are all normal—and, in time, this too shall pass. One day in the near future, the ideas of changing diapers and warming a breast milk bottle will seem as easy to you as booting up a PC or setting the alarm on your smartphone. And then you will know that you have truly mastered baby ownership.

Good luck—and enjoy your new baby!

OTHER ACCESSORIES (not included)

Keep these on hand for the installation, handling, and maintenance of your new baby.

Bottles

Formula

Cereal

Sippy Cups

Pacifiers

Sponges

Soap

Towels & Blankets

Shampoo

Creams

Barrier Cream

Lotions

Baby Wipes

Diapers

Outfits

Head Gear

Toys

The Baby:
Diagram and Parts List

Virtually all current models come pre-installed with the following features and capabilities. If the baby is missing one or more of the functions described herein, contact the baby's service provider immediately.

The Head

Head: May initially appear unusually large or even cone-shaped, depending on model and delivery option. A cone-shaped head will become more rounded after four to eight weeks.

Circumference: The average head circumference of all models is 13.8 inches (35 cm). Any measurement between 12.9 and 14.7 inches (32–37 cm) is considered normal.

Hair: Not available upon delivery with every model. Tint may vary.

Fontanels (Anterior and Posterior): Also known as "soft spots." Fontanels are two gaps in the baby's skull where the bones have not grown together. Never apply pressure to the fontanels. They should seal completely by the end of the first year (or soon after).

Eyes: Most Caucasian models are delivered with blue or gray eyes, while African and Asian models are usually delivered with brown eyes. Be aware that the pigmentation of the iris may change several times during the first few months. The baby will automatically settle on an eye color by the age of nine to twelve months.

Neck: Upon arrival, this feature may appear "useless." This is not a defect. The neck will become more useful in two to four months.

The Body

Skin: The baby's skin may be exceptionally sensitive to the chemicals found in new (unwashed) garments. The skin may react poorly to the chemicals in ordinary laundry detergent. Consider switching to a fragrance-free, chemical-free detergent for all of the laundry in the household.

Umbilical Stump: This appendage will become scabbed and, after several weeks, will fall off. It must be kept clean and dry to avoid infection and to form a healthy navel (see page 212).

Rectum: This is the site of the baby's solid waste output. A thermometer placed in this port will measure the baby's core temperature, which should be approximately 98.6 degrees Fahrenheit (37°C) (see page 194).

Genitals: It is normal for the baby's genitals to appear slightly enlarged. This has no reflection on the future size or shape of the baby's genitals.

Fuzz: Many models come pre-installed with lanugo, a downy coating of hair on the shoulders or back. This coating will disappear within a few weeks.

Weight: The average model weighs 7.5 pounds (3.4 kg) on delivery. The majority weigh between 5.5 and 10 pounds (2.5–4.5 kg).

Length: The average model is 20 inches (51 cm) long on delivery. The majority are between 18 and 22 inches (45–56 cm) long.

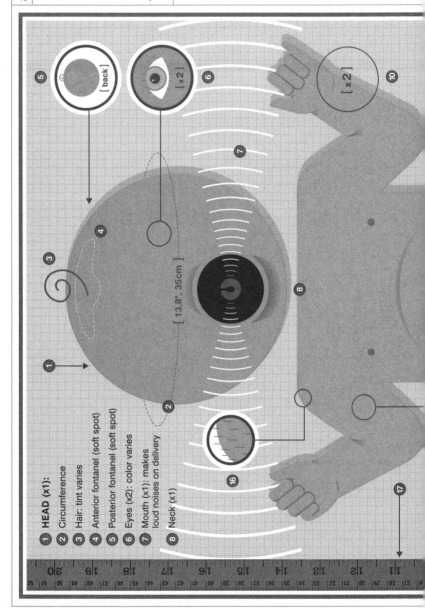

HEAD (x1):

1. Circumference
2. Hair: tint varies
3. Anterior fontanel (soft spot)
4. Posterior fontanel (soft spot)
5. Eyes (x2): color varies
6. Mouth (x1): makes loud noises on delivery
7. Neck (x1)

[back]

[x2]

[x2]

[13.8", 35cm]

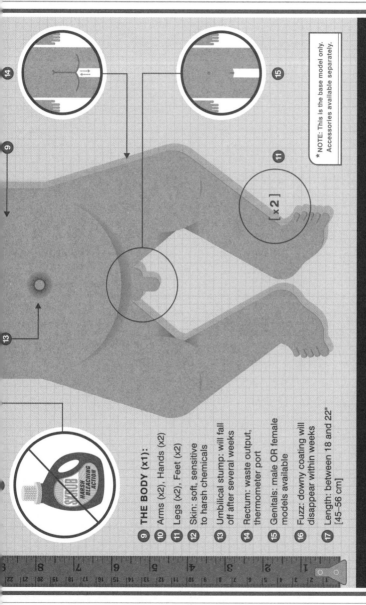

* NOTE: This is the base model only. Accessories available separately.

BABY PARTS LIST: Check your model carefully. If any parts are missing, notify your service provider immediately.

9 THE BODY (x1):

10 Arms (x2), Hands (x2)

11 Legs (x2), Feet (x2)

12 Skin: soft, sensitive to harsh chemicals

13 Umbilical stump: will fall off after several weeks

14 Rectum: waste output, thermometer port

15 Genitals: male OR female models available

16 Fuzz: downy coating will disappear within weeks

17 Length: between 18 and 22" [45–56 cm]

[x 2]

SCRUB — HARSH BLEACHING ACTION

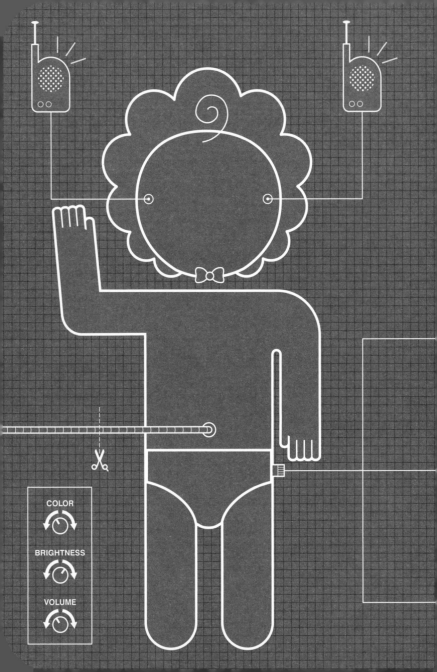

COLOR

BRIGHTNESS

VOLUME

Chapter 1

Preparation and Home Installation

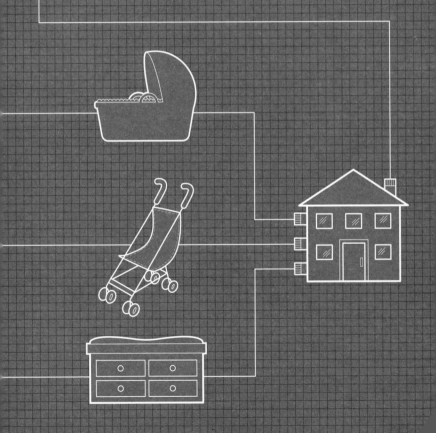

Preparing the Home

A newborn baby has limited mobility, so there is no immediate need to childproof the environment (see page 182). However, it is recommended that you make the following preparations before the baby's arrival.

[1] Finish any home improvement projects well in advance of delivery. The demands of a newborn can delay the completion of these projects for years or even decades.

[2] Adjust and monitor the house temperature. During the first few months of life, the baby will need help regulating internal temperature. The optimal home temperature for a newborn is 68–72 degrees Fahrenheit (20–22°C).

[3] Clean the home thoroughly. Put objects away when you are finished with them. Clean the kitchen after meals. The delivery of the baby may be a surprise. It is helpful to be prepared.

[4] Increase your food supply. Fill the pantry with dry goods. Accumulate frozen late-night snacks. Once you own a baby, navigating the aisles of a grocery store will be infinitely more complicated.

[5] Pre-cook meals. By cooking meals in advance and freezing them, you will have an ample source of food that can last for weeks after the baby's arrival.

⚠ *EXPERT TIP: In the final four weeks before the baby's arrival, never let the gas tank in the automobile dip below half-full.*

Configuring the Baby's Nursery

Most users will choose to keep the baby in a special room of her own. This room is usually referred to as a *nursery*. It is highly recommended that you configure the nursery before your model is delivered. Organization is critical because you may need to find objects and tools at a moment's notice.

The Crib

The crib is the most important object in the nursery. Its location should be safe, comfortable, and accessible—in that order.

Safe: The crib should be away from windows, heat/air conditioning ducts, radiators, loose-hanging items such as curtain cords, and heavy objects such as framed pictures or lamps. The crib should rest atop a soft carpet or throw rug.

Comfortable: The baby might have an increased sense of security if the crib is located in the corner of a room. The crib should not be placed in direct sunlight.

Accessible: The ideal crib is visible from the door to the room, so users can monitor the baby's status at a glance.

For more information on selecting the ideal crib, see page 108.

The Changing Station/Dresser

The *changing station*—which also comes in the form of a combination *changing station/dresser*—is a flat surface, about waist high, that aids in performing diaper removal and reinstallation. Like the crib, an effective changing station will be safe, comfortable, and accessible, and will be configured so that all of your changing supplies are within reach.

⚠ *CAUTION: Never leave the baby unattended on a changing station. This may lead to serious injury and/or malfunction.*

Safe: A crawling baby may grab the face of the changing station in an attempt to pull herself up to a standing position. By fastening the station to the wall with safety brackets, you can ensure its upright position. The changing station should not be placed near radiators, curtain cords, or other hazards.

Comfortable: Many users will lay a foam changing pad on the changing station's surface to cushion the baby and increase her comfort level. These changing pads are usually accompanied by fitted rubber sheets and can be covered with cotton sheets.

Accessible: The ideal changing station location is within an arm's length of extra supplies, extra clothes, a waste disposal, and a laundry hamper.

Other Nursery Items

Rocker or Chair: Place this object in the corner of the room to avoid wasting valuable play space. On a small table beside the rocker, store a soft cloth for burping, a lamp with a dimmer, a book to read, a clock to time feedings, and a warm blanket.

Toy Chest: If space is limited, consider a low toy chest that can slide under the baby's crib.

Humidifier: If you keep a humidifier in the nursery, place it at least four feet from the crib. Mist on the crib may allow bacteria to grow.

Thermostat: It is recommended that users have a thermostat in the nursery, since different rooms of a home often have different temperatures. The ideal temperature for the baby's nursery is 68 degrees Fahrenheit (20°C).

Space Heater: If you have a space heater in the nursery, keep it away from the crib and all flammable materials. Do not leave a space heater on unattended.

Sleep Monitor: This device can be used to monitor the baby's audio output or sleep mode functionality from anywhere in the house. The transmitter is usually left on at all times and should be placed near an electrical outlet. Avoid using extension cords if possible.

Nightlight: Place a small nightlight near or below the baby's crib, out of the baby's line of vision.

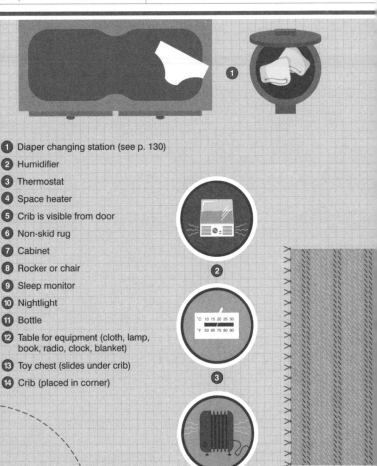

1. Diaper changing station (see p. 130)
2. Humidifier
3. Thermostat
4. Space heater
5. Crib is visible from door
6. Non-skid rug
7. Cabinet
8. Rocker or chair
9. Sleep monitor
10. Nightlight
11. Bottle
12. Table for equipment (cloth, lamp, book, radio, clock, blanket)
13. Toy chest (slides under crib)
14. Crib (placed in corner)

CONFIGURING THE NURSERY: It is important to configure and organize

the nursery before your model is delivered to avoid confusion and frustration.

Essential Baby Accessories

All models require a wide range of accessories, from sleeping supplies to grooming equipment. Listed below are the most essential accessories required during the baby's first month. It is recommended that you purchase most of these items before your model is delivered.

SLEEPING SUPPLIES

- 2 sets of fitted crib or bassinet sheets
- 4–6 receiving blankets
- crib bumper

CHANGING SUPPLIES

- wipes, alcohol free
- barrier cream
- diaper cream
- lotion
- cotton swabs
- 36–60 cloth diapers with six pins and six over-pants

OR

- 1–2 packages of newborn disposable diapers

FEEDING SUPPLIES

- 6–12 burp cloths
- 2 nursing bras
- 4 nursing pads
- lanolin ointment
- 4–6 4-ounce (118 ml) bottles and newborn nipples
- nipple shields

- breast pump with storage bottles and bags (optional

OR

- one-week supply of newborn formula (optional)

CLOTHING SUPPLIES

- 5–7 one-piece undershirts
- 3–5 one-piece shirt/pant suits
- 3–5 one-piece flame-retardant pajamas
- 3–5 flame-retardant nightshirts
- 3–5 pairs of socks
- no-scratch hand mittens
- 2–3 hats
- fleece suit, sweater, and coat (depending on climate)

BATHING AND GROOMING SUPPLIES

- small plastic bathtub
- 2–3 hooded towels
- 2–3 washcloths
- baby bath soap
- baby shampoo
- grooming kit with nail clippers
- nasal bulb

Essential Transportation Accessories

Baby owners require special accessories to transport the baby. Use the following guidelines to select equipment that suits your current lifestyle.

Carriers

A carrier allows users to carry the baby on their person with a reduced amount of effort. Consider your comfort as well as the baby's; if you do not enjoy wearing the carrier, you are not likely to use it.

Front Pack (Fig. A): This carrier—consisting of shoulder straps for the user and a harness for the baby—allows the baby to be supported on the user's chest. The baby should ride "face-in" until she has developed adequate neck strength. Front packs can accommodate babies up to approximately age six months.

Sling/Wrap (Fig. B): These carriers—usually made of soft cotton, nylon, or Lycra—strap over one shoulder or wrap around a user's torso and may be used for infants and older babies. Slings and/or wraps can accommodate babies up to and beyond twelve months.

Backpack (Fig. C): This carrier—usually a metal or plastic frame with soft cotton or nylon padding—allows the baby to ride on the user's back. The baby will need substantial neck and back strength to ride in a backpack; they are not recommended for models younger than six to nine months. Choose an adjustable model that includes a sunshade and storage pockets.

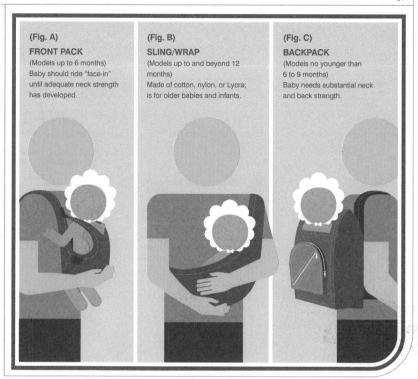

(Fig. A)
FRONT PACK
(Models up to 6 months)
Baby should ride "face-in" until adequate neck strength has developed.

(Fig. B)
SLING/WRAP
(Models up to and beyond 12 months)
Made of cotton, nylon, or Lycra; is for older babies and infants.

(Fig. C)
BACKPACK
(Models no younger than 6 to 9 months)
Baby needs substantial neck and back strength.

Strollers

A stroller allows users to move the baby on casters from point A to point B. Before selecting one, consider its durability, versatility, size, weight, and cost. All primary users should "test drive" the stroller before purchasing it.

Look for the following features when selecting a stroller: five-point harness, storage pockets, cup holders, sun guard, seat padding, rain cover, multi-position front wheels, multi-position seat backs, shock absorbers, and sturdy plastic (or durable air-tube) wheels.

Model:
STANDARD STROLLER

Wheels: 4 or 8

Lifespan: Until baby reaches
40–45 pounds (18–20 kg)

Weight of Stroller:
Average to heavy

Collapsible: Yes

Adaptability: Most can link
with infant car seats

Versatility: 2–4 seat positions

Terrain: Sidewalks, smooth
roads, most indoor surfaces

Model:
JOGGING STROLLER

Wheels: 3

Lifespan: Until baby reaches
35–45 pounds (16–20 kg)

Weight of Stroller:
Average to heavy

Collapsible: Yes

Adaptability: Some can link
with infant car seats

Versatility: 1–2 seat positions

Terrain: Sidewalks, roads,
indoor surfaces, grass trails

STROLLERS: All primary users should "test drive" the stroller before purchasing

Model:
LIGHTWEIGHT STROLLER

Wheels: 4 or 8

Lifespan: Until baby reaches
30–45 pounds (13–20 kg)

Weight of Stroller: Light

Collapsible: Yes

Adaptability: None

Versatility: 1–3 seat positions

Terrain: Indoor surfaces and
smooth sidewalks

Model:
FRAMELESS STROLLER

Wheels: 4

Lifespan: Until baby reaches
20–25 pounds (9–11 kg)

Weight of Stroller: Light

Collapsible: Yes

Adaptability: Designed to link
with infant car seats

Versatility: None

Terrain: Indoor surfaces and
smooth sidewalks

quire about added features (cup holders, sun guards, storage pockets, etc.).

Car Seats

To transport the baby in an automobile, you need a car seat custom-designed for the baby's size. Most newborns are compatible with two different types of car seats: the infant seat and the infant-toddler convertible. Each has its own benefits. Regardless of your selection, read the seat manual carefully and be sure to install the seat properly (see page 35).

Look for the following features: a five-point safety harness, newborn head support, adjustable seat belt, retractable sunshade, comfortable cushioning, and (for convertible seats only) a seat-to-car tether. If you have any concerns, call the manufacturer.

Infant Seat (Fig. A): The primary benefit of the infant seat is that it can be removed from the automobile with the baby in it. It can link to most standard and frameless strollers (see page 31), and is designed to close like a clamshell in the event of an accident. Unfortunately, a fully loaded infant seat weighs nearly 30 pounds (13 kg) and will require safety checks each time you place it in the automobile. The seat will need to be replaced when the baby grows larger than 20 to 25 pounds (9–11 kg), or when she exceeds a length of 26 inches (66 cm).

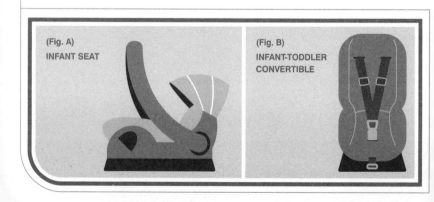

(Fig. A)
INFANT SEAT

(Fig. B)
INFANT-TODDLER
CONVERTIBLE

Infant-Toddler Convertible (Fig. B): Larger than the infant seat, the infant-toddler convertible will last until the baby is approximately four to five years old. Because this seat is not designed to be removed from the automobile, you will need additional carriers upon reaching your destination.

⚠ **EXPERT TIP:** *In general, it is unsafe to purchase a used car seat. Safety regulations change frequently, and old models may be obsolete. If the pre-owned car seat was ever in a car accident, it may no longer function at peak capacity.*

Installing a Car Seat

By law in the United States, all baby models must be safely restrained when riding in an automobile. Until the baby is 12 months old and weighs 20 pounds (9 kg), she must be seated facing the rear of the vehicle. When possible, position the baby in the center of the back seat.

[1] Always defer to the car seat manufacturer's instructions. They will provide contact information if you are having difficulty with the installation.

[2] Obey safety standards. The seat should not be in the path of an airbag or facing a fold-down rear seat armrest. Front automobile seats should never recline against the infant seat; in the event of an accident, this will prevent the device from sealing shut.

[3] Use two people to ensure a secure fit when installing the seat. One person can rest a knee on the car seat, forcing it down, while the other person tightens the seat belts.

[4] Perform safety checks. The car seat should not move more than one inch forward, backward, or side-to-side. Belts should be installed in the proper notches. Attach a locking clip if necessary. The seat should recline at the proper angle (about 45 degrees).

[5] Check the seat's harness straps. They should be flat (not twisted), snugly secure, and firmly attached at snap points.

[6] Support the baby's head. Use the seat's head support or wrap a towel around the top and side of the baby's head. Be sure this support does not interfere with the seat's straps.

[7] Check the seat's stability and safety on a regular basis.

⚛ *EXPERT TIP: Many hospitals, fire stations, and retailers of baby merchandise will inspect and confirm proper car seat installation free of charge.*

Getting to Know the Baby's Service Provider

All models will require the assistance of a service provider known as a pediatrician. Set up a face-to-face interview with the service provider. Consider asking the following questions:

■ *What is your child rearing philosophy?* Some service providers may have specific philosophies, while others may be open to multiple views. Know which philosophy your provider subscribes to, and how it is similar to or different from your own.

■ *Will you see the baby every time we have an appointment?* Some hospitals or clinics have multiple service providers on staff. In an ideal situation, you will see the same service provider on every visit.

■ *Who will treat the baby if you are unavailable?* It is normal for a service provider to have associates work for him or her from time to time. It is also normal for you to ask about their qualifications.

■ *Do you schedule well-child and sick-child visits at different times? Do you have separate waiting rooms for well and sick children?* This will limit the baby's exposure to sick children.

■ *What are your office hours?* This is particularly important if both parents work full time. Some service providers have flexible hours.

■ *Is there a specific hour that you devote to phone calls, or do you take calls throughout the day?* Most service providers will do one or the other. Understanding this policy from the beginning will prevent confusion and frustration in the long run.

■ *Does your nurse or assistant give shots?* Most models will come to fear the person who gives them shots. It is preferable if the service provider has a nurse or assistant perform this task.

In the United States, where users can choose their service providers from a wide pool, it is recommended that you set up interviews with a few doctors who accept your insurance. Secure recommendations from friends, family, and co-workers. Choose a service provider with whom you feel most comfortable, based on the interview.

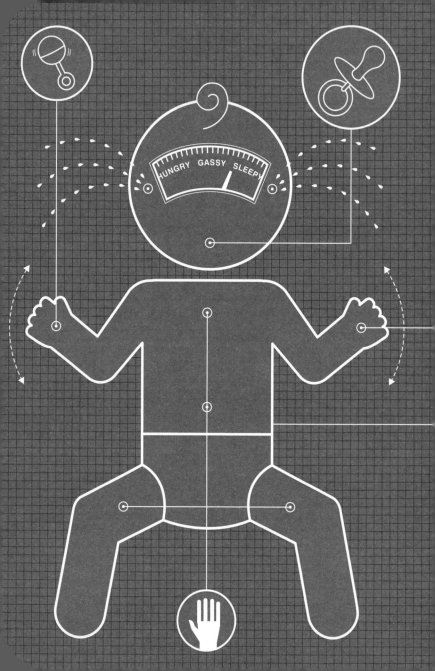

Chapter 2

General Care

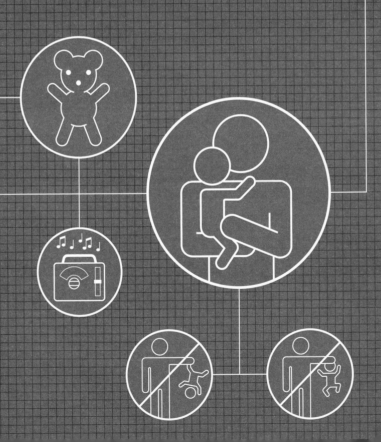

Bonding with the New Baby

It is recommended that users bond with the baby shortly after delivery. Often, this bond will develop instantaneously. In other cases, the baby and the user will require a little more time. No two baby models are alike, and there is no right or wrong way for bonding to occur. However, if you do not feel bonded with the baby after three to four weeks, it is recommended that you discuss this issue with the baby's service provider.

[1] Feel, see, and smell the baby at the first opportunity. If the baby's health allows, ask the nurse, midwife, or doctor to place the baby on your chest immediately after delivery.

[2] Mothers who choose to breastfeed should do so as soon as possible (see page 74). Breastfeeding releases hormones that help contract the uterus, limiting postpartum bleeding. The physical act of breastfeeding may also accelerate the growth of the bond between mother and child. The breast milk provides innumerable health benefits to the baby (see page 72).

[3] Keep the baby with you. If the baby's health allows, arrange to keep the baby in your room. Speak or sing to her. She may recognize the sound of your voice.

⚠ *CAUTION: Take your time. Some mothers will need to take these steps slowly. If you need to recover from the trauma of the delivery before keeping constant contact with the newborn, do so. It is important for the mother and the baby to be together—but it is even more important for the mother to be ready. Nurses, other parents, or family members may supervise the baby while the mother recovers.*

Handling the New Baby

Always wash your hands before handling the baby. Human skin contains bacteria that, when transferred to the baby, can cause him to function improperly. If you do not have access to soap and water, disinfect your hands with a baby wipe.

Picking Up the Baby

[1] Slide one hand under the baby's neck and head to support them (Fig. A). In the first weeks, the baby's neck has minimal function. Until it strengthens, handle the baby with care to prevent undesirable "flopping" of the head.

[2] Slide your other hand under his bottom and spine (Fig. B).

[3] Lift the baby close to your body (Fig. C).

⚠️ *CAUTION: When laying the baby down, always support the baby's head with your hands, and ensure that the surface you put him on will support his head and neck.*

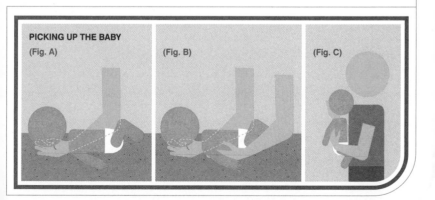

PICKING UP THE BABY
(Fig. A)   (Fig. B)   (Fig. C)

The Cradle Hold

By cradling the baby with his head on the left side of your body, you will expose his ears to an audible rhythmic thumping produced by your heart. Upon receiving this signal, the baby is likely to enter sleep mode (see page 116). This is considered normal—and, for many users, desirable. (The hold can also be performed on the right side.)

[1] Place your right hand under the baby's head and neck. Your left hand should support the baby's bottom and spine (Fig. A).

[2] Guide the baby's head and neck into the crook of your left arm. Your right hand is now free to perform other tasks, while your left hand supports the baby (Fig. B).

[3] For a more secure hold, tuck your right arm under your left arm.

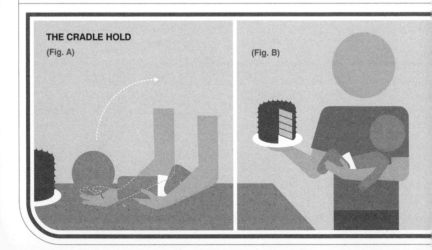

THE CRADLE HOLD
(Fig. A)

(Fig. B)

The Shoulder Hold

This position is ideal for new baby owners. However, as the baby ages, he may no longer enjoy being held in this manner.

[1] Raise the baby so his head rests on the front of your shoulder. His head should not be hanging over your shoulder (Fig. A).

[2] Use the crook of your arm to support the baby's bottom. His legs will hang below this arm.

[3] For a more secure hold, keep your free hand on the baby's back (Fig. B). If you must lean forward at any point, support the baby's head and neck.

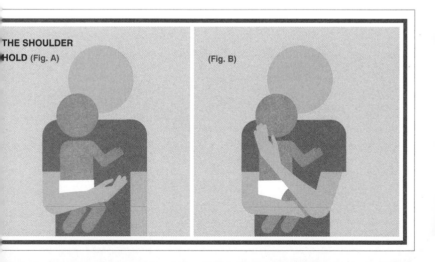

THE SHOULDER HOLD (Fig. A)

(Fig. B)

Passing the Baby

During the baby's first two months of life, the immune system is extremely fragile. It is recommended that you limit the number of visitors during this period. Before passing the baby to another person, be sure this person has washed his or her hands.

When one user wishes to pass the baby off to another, or when friends and family come to visit, use the following techniques to keep the baby safe.

[1] Use one hand to support the baby's head and neck. Your other hand should support the baby's bottom and spine.

[2] Have the other person cross his or her arms.

[3] Set the baby's head and neck in the crook of one arm. Instruct the other person to support the baby's head (Fig. A).

[4] Place the baby's body into the crossed arms (Fig. B).

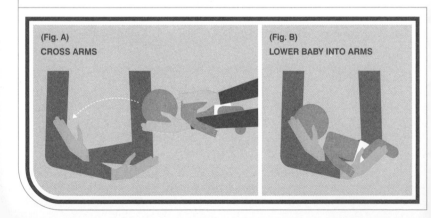

(Fig. A)
CROSS ARMS

(Fig. B)
LOWER BABY INTO ARMS

Holding a Crawling Baby

Crawling babies, generally older than six months, will weigh consider-ably more than when first delivered. The added weight renders previ-ous holding methods obsolete. If the baby is crawling, the muscles in the head, neck, and back have strengthened, making new holding po-sitions viable.

The Hip Hold

[1] Reach your arm around the baby, across her back and under both of her armpits (Fig. A).

[2] Place your free hand on the baby's bottom (Fig. B).

[3] Raise the baby to hip-level on the same side as the arm that is sup-porting her back (Fig. C).

[4] Set the baby on your hip. Many users need to angle their bodies so the hip sticks out, providing additional surface area for the baby to rest on. The baby should be straddling your side with one leg in the front and one leg in the back (Fig. D).

[5] Hold your arm across the baby's shoulder blades. If the baby grabs onto you, you may lower your arm across her lower back.

THE HIP HOLD

(Fig. A)
DOMINANT HAND GOES UNDER BACK

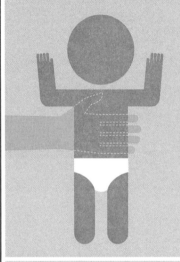

(Fig. B)
OTHER HAND SUPPORTS BOTTOM

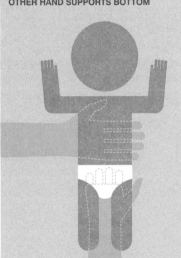

(Fig. C)
RAISE MODEL TO HIP LEVEL

(Fig. D)
SET MODEL ON HIP

The Potato-Sack Hold

Use this hold for short-distance transfers. Since it requires you to hold the baby horizontally, most babies will not tolerate it for long periods of time.

[**1**] Approach the baby from behind.

[**2**] Slide your dominant arm under the baby, between her legs and up to the front, bending your elbow as necessary. Rest your hand on her chest (Fig. A).

[**3**] Place your other hand on her back to stabilize her on your arm (Fig. B).

[**4**] Lift the baby and tuck her into your side. Your non-dominant hand should continue to stabilize the baby (Fig. C).

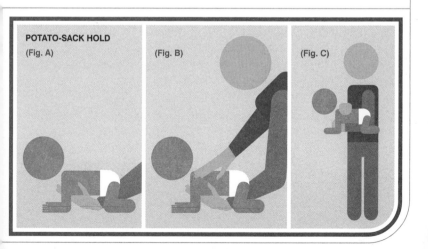

POTATO-SACK HOLD
(Fig. A) (Fig. B) (Fig. C)

Crying: Troubleshooting the Baby's Audio Cues

The baby's audio output system includes two lungs, vocal chords, and a mouth. The baby will use these features to communicate. Since most models do not come with verbal language facility pre-installed, your model's first attempts at communication may sound meaningless. This is a common misconception among new users. These audio cues, called *cries*, often contain a great deal of information for users.

A baby will cry if his diaper is wet or soiled, and if he is hungry, too hot or too cold, tired, gassy, in need of love or comfort, or sick. Some models may cry to hear the sound of their own voices. When your model cries, the pitch and frequency of the cry provide clues to the meaning. Different causes can trigger different types of cries. When the source of a cry has been determined, users should make a mental note of the type of cry, so that future cries of that type can be immediately understood.

Wet or Soiled Diaper: The user's olfactory system should sense when the baby's diaper is soiled, or it can be manually checked by inserting one finger and feeling for wetness. Reinstall the diaper as necessary (see page 132) and see if crying ceases.

Hungry: The baby might feel hungry between seven and ten times a day. Offer food to the baby. He may require a moment to quiet down before eating. If crying ceases, hunger was the probable cause.

Too Hot or Too Cold: Most models are more likely to cry when they are too cold rather than too hot. The baby's internal temperature may rise, but there is no alert system in place to warn the user. Check the status of the baby's clothing and adjust accordingly. Carefully monitor other external signs to determine if the baby may be too hot. Check for flushed, clammy skin. Do not overdress the baby.

Tired: The baby might rub his eyes, yawn, or appear drowsy while crying and might need to enter sleep mode. See the instructions for activating sleep mode on page 116.

Gassy: If the baby is squirming or raising his legs toward his belly, excess gas might be in the digestive system. Burp the baby (see page 94) or hold the baby in a way that will expel the gas (see colic, page 201).

Love or Comfort: If the baby feels that he has been left alone for too long, or if overstimulation has led to confusion, the baby may need to be hugged and comforted by one of the primary users. Try installing a pacification tool, natural or artificial, into the mouth port (see page 55).

Sickness: If the baby is experiencing a malady, the discomfort might lead to crying. Check first to see if the cause is not one of the above reasons. If the crying continues unabated for more than 30 minutes, consult the baby's service provider.

⚠ CAUTION: *Sometimes the source of the baby's cry is difficult to trouble-shoot. Do your best to understand the cry and to remain calm.*

Comforting the Baby

There are various techniques the user may perform to comfort the baby.

[1] Swaddle the baby. Follow the instructions below. The baby may be comforted by the warmth and security that swaddling provides.

[2] Rock the baby. Sit with the baby in a rocking chair, place the baby in a sling, or simply rock your body back and forth while holding her. The steady and smooth rhythms may soothe her.

[3] Bounce the baby. Be very gentle. Rock side to side slightly.

⚠ *CAUTION: Never shake a baby. Bouncing should be gentle and purposeful. Shaking can lead to malfunction.*

[4] Sing to the baby. Her auditory sensors are very receptive to music.

[5] Alter the baby's environment. A change in light or temperature may stop the crying. Consider taking a walk in a stroller or carrier.

[6] Install a pacification tool, natural or artificial (see page 55).

Swaddling the Baby

Swaddling consists of snugly wrapping the baby in a blanket. Your model might appear soothed by feelings of warmth and security, or frustrated by her sudden lack of mobility. Try the techniques listed on the following page, and gauge your model's reaction.

⚠ **CAUTION:** *Since swaddling is confining and may restrict a baby's motor development, a full-body swaddle is not recommended after the baby's first 60 days. When the baby has reached this age, it is best to use a version that leaves her arms unrestricted, such as an altered Burrito Roll (see page 54).*

Quick Wrap

The Quick Wrap is an effective technique for users with a minimum amount of time. Use a blanket that will cover the baby's entire body.

[1] Lay a square blanket on a flat surface.

[2] Fold one corner of the blanket down about the length of your hand.

[3] Lay the baby on the blanket diagonally so the fold is above the top of the baby's neck (Fig. A).

[4] Pull the right side of the blanket across the baby's body. Tuck it under the baby's left side (Fig. B).

[5] Pull the left side of the blanket across the baby's body. Tuck it under the baby's right side (Fig. C).

[6] Lift the baby and tuck the bottom tail of the blanket under the baby's legs and back (Fig. D).

QUICK WRAP

Fig. A

Fig. B

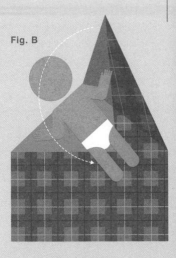

Fig. C

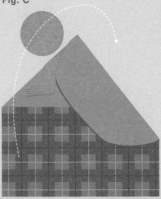

Fig. D

SWADDLING THE BABY: If rocking, bouncing, singing, changing the

BURRITO ROLL

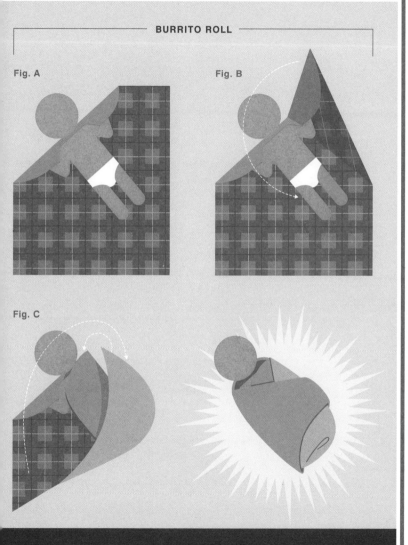

Fig. A

Fig. B

Fig. C

environment, or installing a pacifier doesn't work, try one of these swaddling methods.

Burrito Roll

The Burrito Roll is a more secure (and longer-lasting) version of the Quick Wrap swaddle. When properly dressed in a Burrito Roll, the baby will resemble a popular Mexican foodstuff that consists of a flour tortilla rolled around a meat or bean filling.

[1] Lay a square blanket on a flat surface. The blanket should be large enough to cover the baby's entire body.

[2] Fold one corner of the blanket down about the length of your hand.

[3] Lay the baby on the blanket diagonally so the fold is above the top of the baby's neck (Fig. A).

[4] Tuck the baby's hands into the fold of the blanket. The hands should rest beside the baby's shoulders or face. (If you have a particularly active baby, you can tuck the blanket under the baby's armpits, so her hands will remain mobile.)

[5] Pull the right side of the blanket across the baby's body. Tuck it under the baby's left side (Fig. B).

[6] Fold the bottom tail of the blanket up (toward the baby's head), covering her feet and legs and overlapping the right-side fold. Tuck the tail under the top right edge (Fig. C).

[7] Pull the left side of the blanket across the baby's body. Tuck it under the baby's right side (Fig. C).

Selecting and Installing a Pacifier

Many users install a pacifier to soothe the baby. Most models derive great pleasure from sucking a pacifier. Natural pacifiers include pinkie fingers, knuckles, and thumbs. Artificial pacifiers are made out of latex or silicone molded to look like a bottle's nipple and are available at retailers world-wide. Both natural and artificial versions are suitable for all models. Neither will cause long-term medical or psychological malfunctions.

⚠️ *EXPERT TIP: Watch for signs of nipple confusion. Artificial pacifiers may cause a baby to forget how to latch onto the mother's breast. During the crucial first two months, we recommend avoiding pacifiers altogether. If during later months the baby experiences this phenomenon, limit or discontinue pacifier use.*

Natural Pacifier

[1] Clip or file the nail on your pinkie finger until it has no sharp edges. The baby will prefer this finger to others on the user's hand.

[2] Wash your hands thoroughly.

[3] Turn your hand palm-side up. Extend your pinkie finger to the baby, keeping remaining fingers folded into your palm.

[4] Place the pinkie finger inside the baby's mouth. Just the tip should touch the roof of the baby's mouth. The finger will naturally fit into the curvature of the upper palate.

[5] Allow the baby to suck on your pinkie. Give the baby control of the pinkie, but be sure that it remains against the roof of the baby's mouth.

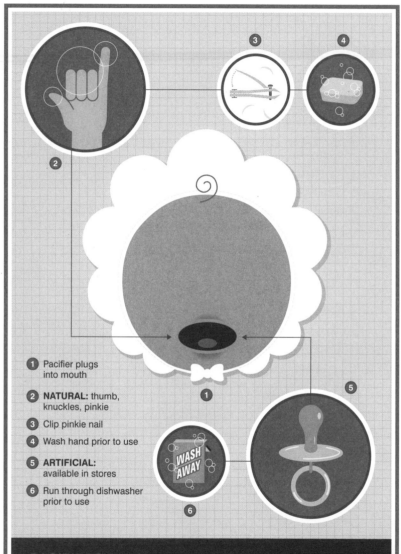

1. Pacifier plugs into mouth
2. **NATURAL:** thumb, knuckles, pinkie
3. Clip pinkie nail
4. Wash hand prior to use
5. **ARTIFICIAL:** available in stores
6. Run through dishwasher prior to use

WASH AWAY

PACIFIERS: Plug one into your model to activate silent mode.

⚠ **EXPERT TIP:** *As the baby ages, encourage her to use her own fingers—or thumbs—for pacifying. If she learns to suck them, she will have a form of pacification wherever she goes.*

Artificial Pacifier

[**1**] Purchase a pacifier from a retailer. Pacifiers come in various shapes and sizes; try several to determine which type is most compatible with your model.

[**2**] Sterilize the pacifier. Put the pacifier through a dishwasher cycle, or submerge it in a pot of boiling water for five minutes. Visually inspect the nipple to be sure no water has leaked through the rubber nipple. If it has, squeeze the water out of the nipple (if possible) or wait for it to evaporate before giving it to the baby.

[**3**] Place the tip of the pacifier inside the baby's mouth.

⚠ **CAUTION:** *Do not tie a pacifier to the baby with a cord or string—this presents a choking and strangulation hazard.*

[**4**] Purchase several pacifiers. Once you have found a pacifier that is compatible with your model, it is recommended that you keep one in her crib, one in the diaper bag, one in the car, one in your pocket, and others in various locations around the house.

[**5**] Replace old pacifiers—especially those with worn-out tips.

⚠ **CAUTION:** *Pacifiers should be used to soothe the baby between feedings, but never in place of them. Without an adequate food supply, the baby will malfunction.*

Massaging the Baby

Many service providers believe that massage can strengthen the immune system, improve muscle development, and stimulate growth of the baby. Massage has a calming effect on most models, and allows the user and baby to develop a closer bond.

The user's hands are the only tools required for massage. Use gentle rubbing and soft, stroking motions. Lay the baby face up on a firm, flat, and comfortable surface. Warm the room and undress the baby if he will allow it. If you massage with oil, opt for a cold-pressed oil such as safflower or almond.

[1] Massage the baby's legs and feet. Begin at the thighs and work your way down to his toes. Rub one leg at a time.

[2] Massage the baby's abdomen. With your hand flat and fingers extended, stroke the baby's abdomen in a circular motion.

⚠ *CAUTION: Massaging the baby's abdomen may trigger emission of urine or gas. Before performing this massage, place a protective washcloth beneath the baby.*

[3] Massage the baby's chest. With your hand flat and fingers extended, stroke the baby's chest. Begin in the middle and move out toward his arms.

[4] Massage the baby's arms and hands. Begin at the shoulders and work your way out toward his fingers. Rub one arm at a time.

[5] Massage the baby's face. Make small circles with your thumbs, then perform light strokes with your fingertips.

MASSAGING THE BABY

FRONT

CAUTION!

Warm the room

CAUTION!

BACK

[6] Turn the baby onto his stomach. Massage the baby's back. Begin rubbing at the shoulders and work your way down both sides of the back. Avoid the spine.

[7] Complete the massage. Turn the baby onto his back and lightly brush your fingers up and down the length of his body. This signals to the baby that the massage is over. If you do not have time for each step, it is recommended that you always perform this final step.

⚠ **EXPERT TIP:** *Infant massage classes are often taught by certified massage instructors. Your local hospital or community center may provide additional information.*

Playing with the Baby

Frequent play time will benefit all models. It serves a trifold purpose: it makes the baby happy, can activate sleep mode, and teaches the baby about his relationship with the world. Find time to play games often.

Music Games

Music is highly recommended during play; it can teach the baby the basics of rhythm, movement, and vocalization, hastening the baby's intellectual and creative development.

[1] Select an appropriate piece of music. Opt for lullabies or other melodic music with only one or two layers of sound. Select songs that have a simple percussive beat.

[2] Play the music.

[3] Dance to the music with the baby. Hold the baby in a way that is appropriate for his neck and back strength. Move your entire body so the baby can feel the rhythm and beat.

[4] Sing to the baby. If you do not know the words, substitute baby talk. The baby may join in.

Strengthening Games

Some forms of play have the added benefit of exercising certain muscles of the baby, which can aid in development. Proper exercise strengthens the baby's muscles, improves the baby's coordination, and increases the baby's motor control.

⚠ *CAUTION: Users should not feel that they need to be a personal trainer to their models—there is no need to exercise the baby. The following movements merely work to strengthen his growing muscles and skills.*

Belly Exercises: Lay the baby facedown on the floor. Lie on the floor next to him and engage him verbally. His responses to you will strengthen his neck, back, and abdominal muscles. He may look up at you, turn his head to look at you, push his body up to see you, or roll himself over.

Sit-Up Exercises: Performing these "sit-ups" is enjoyable to many models and has the added benefit of strengthening abdominal and neck muscles, making unassisted sitting up easier. While sitting down, lay the baby faceup on your lap with his head on your knees. Keeping his legs straight on your lap, place one hand under each armpit and bend him at the waist, bringing his upper body into a vertical position. For older babies, hold his hands and forearms and pull toward you. Repeat.

⚠ **CAUTION:** *Until the baby is at least one year old, do not lift him up by the feet or hands. This could cause a malfunction in his joints.*

Stand-Up Exercises: Many models find this simple move enjoyable, as they can look directly at your face and play with their legs. It has the added benefit of strengthening leg and back muscles. Sit with the baby sitting on your thighs facing you. For younger babies, place both hands under his armpits, raise him to a standing position, and lower him back down to a sitting position. For older babies, lift from the waist, raise the baby to a standing position, and lower him down again.

Selecting Toy Accessories

The use of toy accessories may or may not be necessary for one-month-old babies, but as the baby becomes more sophisticated, toys become vital to mental stimulation. Select toys that are appropriate for the baby's age; refer to the manufacturer's guidelines. The baby's limited comprehension of danger makes it important to avoid toys with sharp edges or loose or small parts. Opt for a stimulating toy; the best accessories will engage two or more of the baby's primary senses (sight, sound, touch, taste, and smell). Choose a book with furry pages, or a scented toy.

Toys for Month 1

Black and White Mobile: Install a mobile with black and white shapes above the crib, just out of reach (about 12 to 15 inches [30–38 cm] above the crib mattress). During early weeks of life, the baby will respond more positively to black and white shapes than to colorful shapes.

Music Player: Use a radio, portable media player, digital audio player, or music box to introduce the baby to music. Studies suggest that higher, calmer, and more melodic music, such as lullabies, will be most appreciated by the baby.

Stuffed Animals: Babies frequently mistake these toys as living, breathing companions (particularly if the stuffed animal has wide eyes). This is a technical glitch that usually disappears within seven to twelve years.

Toys for Months 2 to 6

⚠ **CAUTION:** *Be sure the toy is safe. All models will begin to place objects in their mouths. Make sure all toys are solidly built, securely sewn, and do not have any loose, small parts. Inspect all toys regularly to ensure they meet these standards.*

Activity Pads: Sold as an accessory at many baby-supply stores, activity pads are floor pads with multiple colors, patterns, and overhanging toys that help the baby learn how to swat at and eventually reach the things that interest him.

Books: Select books that the baby can explore with all of his senses. Board books, cloth books, and foam books are all useful tools for getting the baby interested in reading. Let him play with these books as he will, whether he chooses to look at them, feel them, or gnaw on them.

Instruments: Many babies enjoy playing and listening to music. Small drums or bells (without sharp edges) can tune the baby's audio sensors.

Mobiles: At six months, the baby has the ability to see colors and to process complex shapes. To help develop his visual sense, choose a hanging or moving mobile with unusual shapes and bright colors. Replace the black and white mobile with a colorful one over the baby's crib or in an area under which the baby can lie down.

Rattles, Squeaky Toys, and Balls: As the baby develops the ability to grab and manipulate objects, give him small handheld toys to enhance these skills. Toys that make sounds will teach the baby the principles of cause and effect.

Unbreakable Plastic Mirror: Place one next to the changing table or attach one firmly to the side of the crib to provide a few minutes of daily entertainment and self-awareness.

⚠ **EXPERT TIP:** *Some of the best (and least expensive) baby toys are everyday household objects such as spoons or coasters. These objects may be familiar to you, but they are new and exciting to the baby. Select objects that are too large to fit in the baby's mouth, and are free of loose parts, sharp edges, or strangulation hazards.*

Toys for Months 7 to 12

Balls: The baby may still enjoy tasting toys, so make sure the balls are too large to fit in his mouth (and too hard to bite a piece out of). As the baby approaches 12 months, he may begin to roll or even throw a ball back to you.

Bath Toys: Rubber objects that float, hold water, squirt, and/or stick to the side of the tub may entertain the baby during cleaning.

Blocks: Wooden and plastic blocks will help the baby learn to place and stack objects. Many models prefer knocking over stacks of blocks to stacking them. This is normal functioning.

Puppetry and Stuffed Animals: Entertain the baby by putting on shows or making his inanimate friends dance and sing.

Pull Toys: These toys often perform in some way when the string is pulled. Playing with these toys will teach the baby basic cause and effect. Always supervise the baby when he is playing with any toy featuring a pull string. He may swallow the string or pull tab.

Walkers: Once the baby is strong enough to pull up on furniture and take a few supported steps, many users purchase a walker. These wheeled items can be used by the baby for support while taking his first few steps. Walkers can be wagons, wheeled chairs, or anything the baby can hold onto and use to propel himself across the floor. Saucer walkers, however, are not recommended.

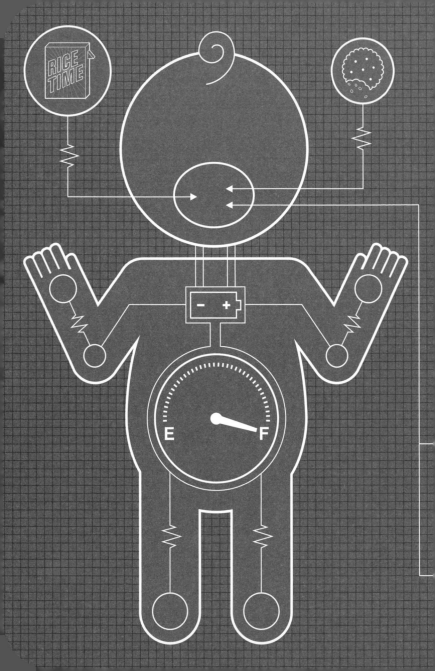

Chapter 3

Feeding: Understanding the Baby's Power Supply

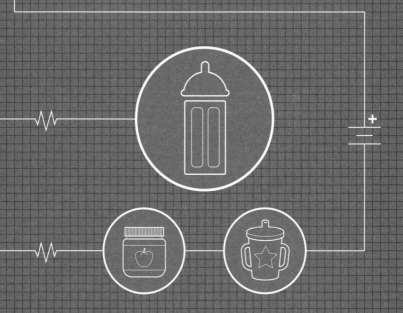

Programming the Baby's Feeding Schedule

There are no definitive guidelines for how much food the baby should consume. Every model is unique and has specific needs. However, extensive studies indicate that most newborns eat two to three ounces (59–88 mL) per feeding, every three to four hours. These habits may fluctuate based on health, activity, growth spurts, and even outdoor weather conditions. As the baby ages, she will require fewer feedings.

Gauging the Baby's Feeding, Month 1

To ensure a proper feeding schedule for your model, be aware of the following three gauges.

Weight Gain: After her first week—during which the baby may lose up to one-tenth of her birth weight—a newborn will generally gain up to one ounce (28 g) per day. If the baby's weight follows this schedule, you can assume the baby is receiving enough food. Note how much weight the baby has gained at the next visit to the baby's service provider. If the baby's weight follows, or closely meets, this schedule, she is most likely receiving the right amount of food.

Physical Cues: The baby's built-in "rooting" reflex (see page 161) can help you gauge appetite. If the baby is hungry, she may activate the rooting reflex—her mouth may open and she may appear to be searching for food.

Diapers: Most well-fed babies will have six to eight wet or soiled diapers every day.

Gauging the Baby's Feeding, Months 2 Through 6

During each model's second through sixth months, breast milk or formula is consumed on a more reliable schedule. By the fourth month, she may be ready to consume simple solid foods such as rice cereal, though many users do not stop breastfeeding at this time. There are no definitive guidelines for how much food the baby should or should not consume. Most models will eat eight times a day, and less frequently with age. If you are concerned about her intake, focus on the following three gauges.

Weight Gain: During this period, the baby will gain about one half to one ounce (14–28 g) per day. Note how much weight the baby has gained at the next visit to the baby's service provider. If the baby's weight follows, or closely meets, this schedule, she is most likely receiving the right amount of food.

Physical Cues: The baby's rooting reflex will evolve into a more purposeful search for food. The baby may attempt to latch onto your arm or suck on her fingers to indicate she is hungry. As a result, it will be easier to tell when the baby is hungry. During this period, the baby will probably cue the user for food every three to four hours.

Diapers: Monitor the baby's diapers to determine if all food has been properly processed. As you introduce the baby to solid foods, the waste will thicken and will adopt the color of the food.

Gauging the Baby's Feeding, Months 7 Through 12

During the seventh to twelfth months, the baby will begin to demand food on a regular schedule. Though the baby's primary diet will be breast milk or formula, begin supplementing the diet with a variety of solid foods: pureed fruits, vegetables, and eventually finger foods, meats, and other proteins.

By the seventh month, users should have a clear sense of how much food the baby requires. If you are concerned about her intake, focus on the following three gauges.

Weight Gain: The baby will gain approximately half an ounce (14 g) per day. This indicates normal functioning and food consumption.

Physical Cues: By this point, the baby's physical cues—crying, gumming objects, and attempting to "eat" her hands—should be very familiar and obvious. Also, the baby's desire for food may begin to coincide with your own personal meal times (though the baby will require additional snacks in between).

Diapers: As you continue introducing the baby to solid foods, her waste will thicken and will resemble the color of her food. Soiled diapers will continue to be a good indication that the food consumption process is working properly.

⚠ **EXPERT TIP:** *In general, the baby will consume approximately six to eight ounces (177–236 mL) of milk four to six times per day, in addition to any solid foods.*

Demand Feeding versus Flexible-Scheduled Feeding

Most users employ one or both of the following techniques to determine if their model requires nourishment.

Demand Feeding: All models come pre-equipped with physical cues to indicate that additional food is necessary. These cues may include (but are not limited to) crying, rooting, and gnawing on hands. Users who employ "demand feeding" offer food upon receiving one of these cues.

Flexible-Scheduled Feeding: Preferred among users with babies older than three months, flexible-scheduled feeding involves offering food every two to four hours (with adjustments based on the baby's sleeping habits, growth conditions, and health). This allows the user to establish a daily routine.

BREAST MILK VERSUS FORMULA:

The baby's first food may be provided through either breast milk or formula. Pediatricians, nurses, midwives, and other service providers in the baby-care industry agree that human milk is the superior food source

Breast Milk

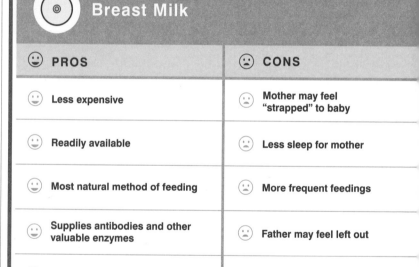

☺ PROS	☹ CONS
☺ Less expensive	☹ Mother may feel "strapped" to baby
☺ Readily available	☹ Less sleep for mother
☺ Most natural method of feeding	☹ More frequent feedings
☺ Supplies antibodies and other valuable enzymes	☹ Father may feel left out
☺ Enhances mother-child bonding	
☺ Aids in postpartum uterine contraction	
☺ Aids in pacification of baby	

Selecting the Baby's Food Source

and will lead a baby to deliver peak performance. However, some users are unable to breastfeed, and others find that it is impractical. Consider the options and choose what works best for you.

Formula

😃 PROS	😦 CONS
😃 Anyone can provide feeding	😦 No antibodies in formula
😃 Fewer feedings required	😦 More expensive
😃 Easy to measure food intake	😦 More equipment required
😃 Easier to feed baby while traveling	😦 More preparation required
😃 No medication or dietary concerns for mother	

Breastfeeding the Baby

The breasts of the male parent are not compatible with the baby's food intake system. If you are the male parent, we recommend that you read this information very carefully and then transfer this section of the manual to the female parent for her review.

The Basics of Breastfeeding

The baby comes pre-loaded with the instincts and skills to begin breastfeeding almost immediately. The baby owner, on the other hand, requires additional training. Familiarize yourself with the following terms.

Colostrum: Breasts produce a thick, orange-yellow fluid during the baby's first days. Colostrum is rich in antibodies, proteins, and protective essentials.

Foremilk and Hind Milk: Breasts usually transfer two different kinds of milk during a single feeding. First, the baby receives foremilk—a thin, watery liquid that satisfies the baby's hydration needs. This is followed by hind milk, which is richer, thicker, and vital to the baby's health and growth.

Let-Down Reflex: When the baby begins to feed, the let-down reflex may activate automatically within the nursing mother. Her body releases hormones that stimulate milk production and release milk from her nipples. Be aware that some mothers never experience the let-down reflex—this is normal.

Engorged Breasts: The mother's breasts may fill in advance to accommodate a feeding schedule, causing a potentially uncomfortable engorgement. The user may relieve the pressure of engorged breasts by feeding the baby, applying a warm or cold compress, or using a breast pump.

EXPERT TIP: *If you use a breast pump to relieve engorgement, do not express more than an ounce (29 mL) at a time. The more milk your body expresses, the more it will produce.*

Essential Breastfeeding Accessories

The following accessories may serve to make breastfeeding easier. All are readily available at your local retailer.

 Breastfeeding Pillows: These specially designed pillows fit around the mother's body and help support the baby during feeding.

 Slings: Some users find that over-the-shoulder carry slings (page 30) provide useful support during breastfeeding.

Comfortable Chairs or Rockers: Chairs that match the mother's body type and sitting style can increase comfort during feeding. Many users enjoy adding an ottoman.

 Nursing Shirts and Bras: Nursing shirts with overlapping slits rather than buttons can make accessing breasts easier. Nursing bras can also provide easy access, as well as dryness protection after feeding. Purchase bras after milk comes in, as breast size will change.

 Breast Pumps and Supplies (optional): A breast pump is a manual or electromechanical device that extracts milk from the user's breasts. The pump enables the female parent to take a break from constant feeding—and provide the male parent with a chance to feed the baby. This accessory is rather expensive; you may opt to rent one from the baby's service provider or a local hospital. It should be used in conjunction with storage bottles and bags and with delivery bottles and nipples.

How to Eat a Good Nursing Diet

The contents of breast milk vary depending on what kinds of food the mother consumes. To give the baby the benefits of a healthy diet—and to guarantee peak performance—follow these guidelines.

[1] Adjust your calorie intake. Users are advised to increase their daily intake by 300 to 500 calories. Ask the baby's service provider if this is necessary for you and your model.

[2] Eat a well-balanced diet. This includes (but is not limited to) several servings of whole grains, cereals, fruits, vegetables, and dairy products daily, as well as plenty of protein, calcium, and iron.

[3] Avoid tobacco, caffeine, and alcohol. Research suggests that smoking tobacco while breastfeeding has a direct correlation to Sudden Infant Death Syndrome (see page 215). Caffeine is acceptable in moderation, but plan accordingly—consume caffeine only after breastfeeding so the caffeine can pass through your system prior to the next feeding. Similar planning is necessary for alcohol consumption—but it is recommend that you avoid beer, wine, and cocktails altogether.

[4] Some users may want to exercise discretion with spicy foods. Milk that is tainted with flavors such as curry, garlic, or ginger will make some models unhappy; others will not notice. Be mindful of when you eat these foods, and note your model's response.

[5] Avoid gassy foods if the baby suffers from colic (see page 201).

[6] Consult the baby's service provider about vitamins, medications, and supplements. Many users continue taking pre-natal vitamins while breast-feeding. Always check with the baby's service provider before taking any supplements or prescription medications.

[7] Drink a minimum of 64 ounces (1.9 L) of water per day.

[8] Avoid weight-loss diets.

⚠ *CAUTION: If you elect to begin a weight-loss diet, consult a service provider to ensure the baby will receive the proper nutrition. Avoid diet pills and plan on losing only one pound per week, balancing a healthy diet with exercise. Wait at least six weeks after the baby's birth before attempting to lose weight. Be aware that most female users will not return to their pre-baby mass until 10 to 12 months after delivery. Also be aware that the act of breastfeeding burns about 300 calories a day.*

[9] Watch for allergy symptoms. If the baby exhibits symptoms such as gas, diarrhea, rash, or general fussiness, he may have a dairy allergy. Eliminate dairy products from your diet for two weeks and see if the baby's condition improves. If it does, present these findings to the baby's service provider.

Breastfeeding Positions

The user may choose to breastfeed the baby in any number of positions. Listed below are three of the most common. Advanced users may modify these positions into a variation that feels most comfortable.

⚠ *EXPERT TIP: Many users undress themselves and the baby before breastfeeding. Increasing the amount of skin-to-skin contact may stimulate both the feeding response and the production of milk.*

Cradle Hold

This general "all-purpose" hold is one of the easiest positions for beginning users to maintain (Fig. A).

[1] Sit in a comfortable seat. Use pillows to support your arms, back, and the baby's weight. Place feet on a footstool, if desired.

[2] Cradle the baby with the head near the breast you wish to use.

[3] Turn the baby so he faces you. Your breast will face the baby's face.

[4] Tuck in the baby's arms to decrease his mobility.

[5] Prompt the baby to latch on (see page 82).

The Football Hold

This hold is often used by mothers recovering from cesarean section, because it prevents the baby from resting on the incision. It can be used with any model, regardless of mode of delivery (Fig. B).

[1] Sit in a comfortable seat. Wedge pillows under your arm and place your feet on a footstool.

[2] Slide one arm under the baby's body, back, and head, so that his feet are between your side and arm. If you are feeding from the left breast, use the left arm. If you are feeding from the right breast, use the right arm. Support the baby's head and neck with your arm.

[3] Turn the baby's body to face your own.

[4] Tuck the baby's torso snugly under your armpit.

[5] Encourage the baby to latch on (see page 82).

Lying Down

This position is most frequently used at night. It is also beneficial if the mother is feeling tired (Fig. C).

[1] Lie down. If you wish to use your left breast, lie on your left side. If you wish to use your right breast, lie on your right.

[2] Place one pillow behind your body, another under your head, and one between your knees.

[3] Place the baby next to your breast. His body should face your body, and his face should be level with your breast.

[4] Place a pillow on the back side of the baby to keep him snug against your body.

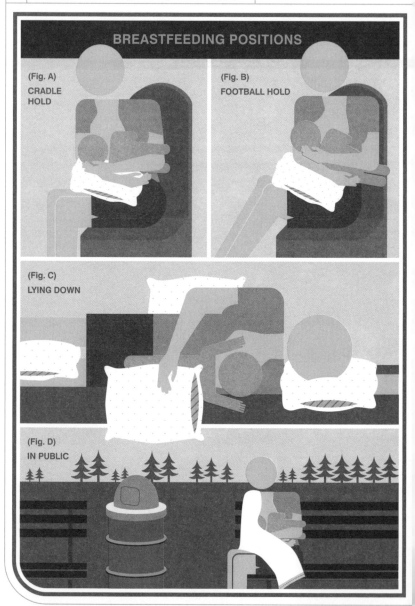

[5] Prompt the baby to latch on (see page 82).

Breastfeeding in Public

Breastfeeding in public is acceptable in most venues. Use the following techniques to make the practice more comfortable (Fig. D).

[1] Find a quiet, comfortable location. If you are outside, find an unpopulated area, preferably with a bench or seat. If you are in a restaurant or department store, ask the hostess or a sales clerk if there is a private area or office available.

[2] Use the cradle or football hold. Spread a blanket over the baby and your shoulder. This blanket functions as a tent, covering the baby's head and your exposed breast. The blanket should not be too heavy or too close to the baby's face.

[3] Begin feeding (see page 82).

[4] Burp the baby (see page 94) with the blanket covering your breast and the baby's body.

[5] When you are ready to switch breasts, move the blanket.

Latching On

A proper latch is essential for good breastfeeding. A weak latch between your model and your breast will lead to inefficient, frustrating, and often painful breastfeeding.

[1] Face the baby toward the breast. This will give the baby a clear view of his food source. The baby's body should be straight from head to toe.

[2] Activate the baby's rooting reflex. Stroke the baby's cheek with a finger; the baby should turn in the direction of the stimulus, his mouth port open and ready to accept food (Fig. A).

[3] Raise the baby's head and body toward the breast. Always bring the baby toward the breast; never bring the breast toward the baby.

[4] Seal the baby's mouth around the nipple and areola. A proper latch will form a tight seal between the baby and breast (Fig. B). The baby's bottom lip should be folded outward. If he only has the nipple and/or part of the areola, the latch may be painful for the mother (and not as satisfying for the baby).

[5] Once he has latched on, move the baby's entire body toward your own. Depending on your position, add additional pillows for increased support (Fig. C).

[6] Feeding should begin automatically. As the baby feeds, the ears will move, and you will hear him swallowing.

[7] To break the latch, insert one finger into the baby's mouth to break the suction, and remove the breast. If the mother wishes to switch breasts, or if the latch was not good, repeat steps 1 through 6.

⚠️ **EXPERT TIP:** *Never touch the back of the baby's head during feeding. This activates a pulling-back reflex that can cause damage to the breast. Hold the baby by the back of the neck, under his ears, so your hand functions as the baby's neck support.*

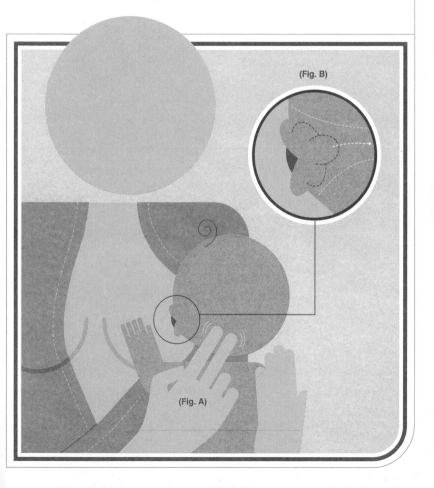

(Fig. B)

(Fig. A)

Alternating Breasts and Proper Feeding Frequency

Ideally, the baby should spend equal time on both breasts during the day—but the exact amount of time on each breast will vary from model to model and from feeding to feeding. Many factors (including growth spurts, frequency, and feeding philosophy) can influence the duration of the feeding. In general, however, we recommend the following guidelines.

⚠ *EXPERT TIP: If you don't produce enough milk for the baby, try to increase the frequency of the feedings. The more stimulation the breasts receive, the more milk they will produce. Consult with the baby's service provider before supplementing breast milk with formula.*

[1] Begin every feeding with the last breast used during the previous feeding. Keep track by affixing a paper clip or safety pin to your bra, or jot a record on a notepad. This will equalize your milk production; many models spend more time on the first breast than the second.

[2] Allow the baby at least 10 to 15 minutes on the first breast. The majority of the milk—both foremilk and hind milk—should be expressed during this time. Let the baby nurse until he pulls off.

[3] Burp the baby (see page 94).

[4] Offer the second breast to the baby and allow him to nurse as long as desired.

[5] Burp the baby (see page 94).

[6] If necessary, install a clean diaper.

[7] Note which breast was used last (see step 1).

⚠ **EXPERT TIP:** *Often, a newborn baby will fall asleep during, or right after, a first-breast feeding. To rouse the baby and continue feeding, try re-installing the diaper or stroking the baby's feet or back.*

Bottle Feeding

Feeding a baby using a bottle is a convenient and easy technique for many users. Users who breastfeed can express the milk, which then can be served to the baby by people other than the mother. Users who do not breastfeed can feed the baby formula from this convenient receptacle. Always choose a shatter-resistant bottle, preferably one that slants near the nipple. This prevents excess air bubbles from collecting near the nipple.

Cleaning Bottles

To protect the baby from contamination, thoroughly wash the feeding equipment daily for the first six months. When you have had the baby for six months, use soap and water daily and sterilize weekly. Sterilize all equipment, including feeding bottles, nipples, storage bottles, and caps.

[1] Wash your hands thoroughly with soap and warm water.

[2] Empty and wash all feeding equipment. Use soap, warm water, and a brush. Clean each piece thoroughly and rinse.

[3] Place all supplies in a large pot filled with water.

[4] Boil the water and the supplies for a minimum of ten minutes. Leave the pot uncovered to prevent the supplies from melting.

[5] Remove the pot from the heat.

[6] Remove the supplies, drain, and allow to air dry.

Storing Breast Milk

[1] Pump the breast milk. Use your breast pump, or express the milk manually into a sterile container, such as a bottle. It is recommended that users stockpile the amount of a full feeding (two to four ounces [59 to 118 mL]) plus a few partial feedings (one to two ounces [29 to 59 mL]).

[2] Seal the container tightly.

[3] Mark the container with the date and time.

[4] Place the container in the refrigerator or transfer its contents to a plastic bag and store in the freezer. Breast milk can remain in the refrigerator for five days—and can be frozen at any point during the five days. Breast milk can remain in the freezer for two to four months.

⚠ *CAUTION: Any breast milk that is thawed after being frozen should be used within 24 hours. Discard any unused milk.*

Warming Stored Breast Milk

[1] If milk was stored in the freezer, thaw it by holding the container under warm (not hot) water, or allow the container to thaw in the refrigerator. Transfer the liquid to a bottle.

[2] Place the bottle in a bowl of warm water until the milk is lukewarm.

⚠ *CAUTION: Do not use a microwave oven to heat breast milk. Microwaves heat liquids unevenly and eliminate valuable enzymes from breast milk.*

[3] Attach a nipple to the bottle.

[4] Gently roll the bottle from side to side. Sometimes, the milk's fat content will separate during warming, and this will mix it back into the liquid. Do not shake the bottle.

[5] Test the temperature of the milk. Shake a few drops of milk onto the underside of your wrist. The milk should be body temperature or cooler. If the milk is too warm, let it cool in the refrigerator.

[6] Serve (see page 90). Discard any unfinished milk.

Formula-Feeding the Baby

There are numerous brands and varieties of formula. The majority of these brands are cow's milk–based formulas, processed to make the milk compatible with the baby. Other formulas can be soy-milk based.

Selecting Formula

Most commercial formulas are available in the following formats. Select a format that works best for your lifestyle.

($$$) Single-Servings: Pre-mixed and packaged in four- and eight-ounce (118 and 236 mL) bottles, these containers are ready upon warming and installation of a sterilized nipple. This is the most convenient and most expensive option.

($$) Liquid Formulas: Available in cans, liquid formula is poured into a sterilized bottle and warmed before serving. This option is moderately convenient and reasonably priced.

($) Mixable Formulas: Available in cans or single-serving packets, mixable formula is a highly concentrated powder (or liquid) that is mixed with sterilized water. The powdered version can be measured into an empty bottle and stored without spoiling until the user adds water, making this option convenient for travel. This requires more effort than other formulas, but it is the most affordable.

Warming Mixable Formula

Mix formula as needed. Do not prepare formula in advance of feedings.

[1] Heat a small amount of water in a clean saucepan until it boils. Follow the instructions on the formula package to determine how much water you need. Some users will use presterilized water, which is available from retailers of baby accessories. This water does not need to be boiled.

[2] Wash your hands thoroughly.

[3] Let the water cool until it is slightly above body temperature.

[4] Pour the required amount of water into the bottle.

[5] Add the formula.

[6] Attach the nipple.

[7] Shake the bottle to mix, keeping one finger (or a cap) over the nipple. Shake until there are no lumps.

[8] Test the temperature of the formula. Shake a few drops onto the underside of your wrist. The formula should be body temperature or cooler. If it is too warm, place it in a refrigerator to cool. If you are using pre-sterilized water, set the bottle in a warm water bath to bring it to a lukewarm temperature.

Preparing Formula on the Go

If you are feeding mixable formula to the baby, always keep a bottle and a few packets of formula in the diaper bag. Most restaurants and coffee shops can provide you with the water you will need.

[1] Ask a server or coffee shop worker for a cup of warm water.

[2] Add the formula and the water to the bottle. Shake vigorously, covering the nipple with one finger or a cap. Be sure there are no lumps in the mixture or in the nipple.

[3] Add some ice chips or cold water to cool the formula to lukewarm.

[4] Test the temperature. Shake a few drops onto the underside of your wrist. The formula should be body temperature or cooler. If it is too hot, add more ice chips.

[5] Serve (see below).

Bottle-Feeding the Baby

Bottle feedings can take place anywhere, anytime. The user can be sitting comfortably or even standing. Always hold the baby upright; lying down increases the baby's risk of choking or getting an ear infection.

[1] Immediately before feeding, hold the bottle nipple under warm water to bring it to body temperature (Fig. A).

[2] Cradle the baby (see page 78). Hold the baby's head slightly above her body (Fig. B).

[3] Activate the baby's rooting reflex. Stroke the baby's cheek with a finger; the baby should turn in the direction of the stimulus, her mouth port open and ready to accept food (Fig. C).

[4] Place the nipple inside the baby's mouth. Aim the nipple so that it touches the roof of the baby's mouth. The baby's lips should point out rather than fold in (Fig. D).

⚠ *EXPERT TIP: Try inserting the nipple one lip at a time. Gently push the baby's top lip upward as you insert the nipple. Push down and out on the baby's bottom lip as you let the nipple settle in her mouth.*

[5] Hold the bottle upright. The milk or formula should completely fill the bulbous region of the bottle. Never prop the bottle so the baby can feed herself. This could lead to injury and/or malfunction.

⚠ *CAUTION: Avoid letting air fill the bulbous region of the nipple. This can cause gas and discomfort.*

[6] Remove the bottle after five to ten minutes, or when empty. Roughly two to three ounces should have been consumed (Fig. E).

[7] Burp the baby (see page 94) (Fig. F).

[8] Resume feeding until the baby consumes a total of several ounces (approximately 100 mL), or appears to be full (Fig. G).

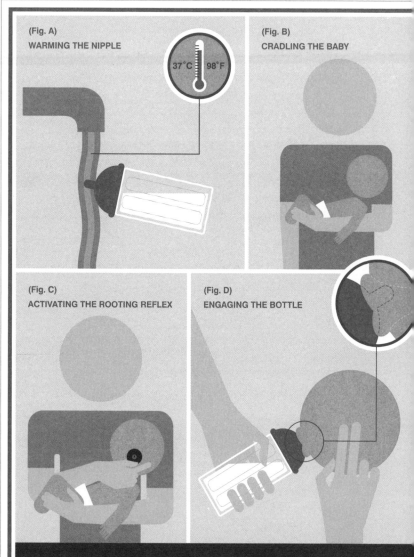

(Fig. A)
WARMING THE NIPPLE

37°C 98°F

(Fig. B)
CRADLING THE BABY

(Fig. C)
ACTIVATING THE ROOTING REFLEX

(Fig. D)
ENGAGING THE BOTTLE

BOTTLE FEEDING: May be done anyplace, anytime. WARNING: Hold mode

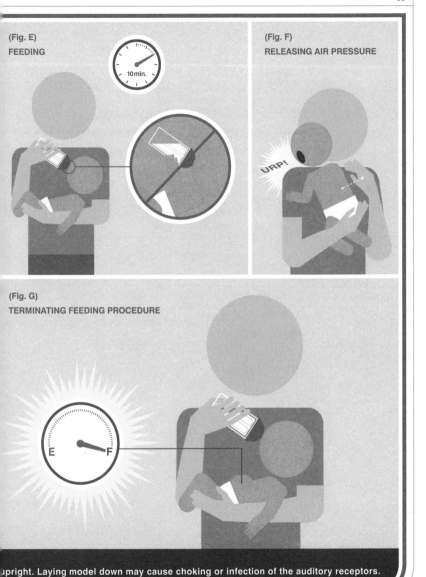

(Fig. E)
FEEDING

10 min.

(Fig. F)
RELEASING AIR PRESSURE

URP!

(Fig. G)
TERMINATING FEEDING PROCEDURE

E F

upright. Laying model down may cause choking or infection of the auditory receptors.

Burping the Baby

Whenever the baby eats, he will swallow air. This air may lead to false feelings of fullness, uncomfortable gas, or the urge to spit up. The user can prevent these consequences by regularly *burping* the baby. During the first few months of operation, burp the baby in the middle and at the end of each feeding. After approximately four months, burp the baby periodically during feedings, particularly after two or three ounces have been consumed from a bottle, or when switching breasts.

EXPERT TIP: *Some babies might have trouble eating after an interruption. If your model experiences such difficulties, wait until the end of the feeding to burp him.*

Use either one of these techniques to burp the baby.

The Shoulder Burp (Fig. A)

[1] Drape a burp cloth or towel over one shoulder.

[2] Hold the baby using the shoulder hold (see page 43).

[3] Rub the baby's back. Make small circles near his shoulder blades. If this does not activate the baby's burping feature, proceed to the next step.

[4] Gently pat the baby's back from his bottom to his shoulder blades.

[5] Repeat steps 3 and 4 for five minutes. If you do not produce a burp in this time, proceed with feeding (or cleanup). The baby should function normally.

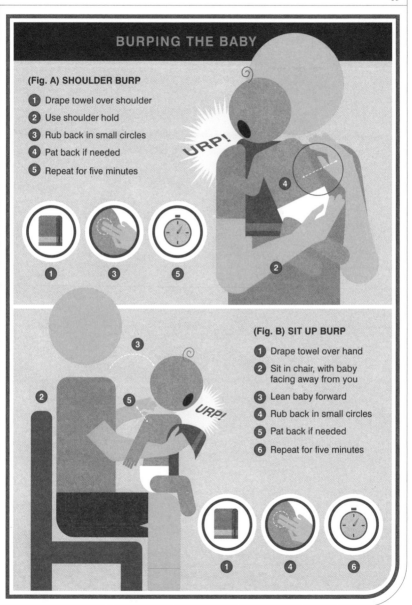

The Sit Up Burp (Fig. B)

[1] Drape a burp cloth or towel over one hand and sit in a chair.

[2] Sit the baby on your lap, facing away from you. Place your free hand on his back. Place the hand with the burp cloth on his chest, supporting the baby's head and neck with your fingers. Lean the baby forward.

[3] Rub the baby's back. Make small circles near his shoulder blades. If this does not activate the baby's burping feature, proceed to the next step.

[4] Pat the baby's back. Gently pat from his bottom toward his shoulders.

[5] Repeat steps 3 and 4 for five minutes. If you do not produce a burp in this time, proceed with feeding (or cleanup). The baby should function normally.

Eliminating Middle of the Night Feedings

The baby will require middle of the night feedings until she is at least nine to twelve months old. By one year, these feedings may be more due to habit than physical necessity. Phase out night feedings in the following way.

[1] Reduce the amount of food administered by small increments. If you are feeding from a bottle, prepare seven ounces (207 mL) the first night, six ounces (177 mL) the second, and so on. If you are breastfeeding, reduce the time the baby feeds by one minute each night.

[2] Observe the baby's daytime eating habits. Most models will make up for the lost night feeding by eating more during waking hours. Eventually she will no longer require any night feedings.

Introducing the Baby to Solid Food

When the baby is sitting up on his own, chewing or biting on objects, and has doubled his birth weight, he may be ready to consume solid food. This usually occurs between the baby's fourth and sixth month. Contact the baby's service provider before introducing the baby to solid food.

Essential Solid-Food Feeding Equipment

The transition from breast milk or formula to solid foods requires the following new equipment.

Small Baby Spoons: These spoons are made of shatterproof plastic. They are small enough to be compatible with the baby's small mouth port and soft enough not to hurt the baby's gums. Two to three of these should be enough.

Baby Bowls: Bowls made especially for the baby are made of shatterproof plastic and hold only a small amount of food.

Bibs: These small pieces of cloth can be tied around the baby's neck to minimize the amount of spit-up or smeared food that gets on the baby's clothing. They are available for purchase at baby supply stores.

Highchair: This accessory will limit the mobility and movement of the baby during feeding. Many different versions are available; most will come with a tray feature upon which food can be placed. Opt for a highchair with sturdy construction.

⚠️ **CAUTION:** *Do not feed the baby in a highchair until the baby can sit up unassisted. Never leave a baby unattended in a highchair.*

Feeding the Baby Solid Food

An ideal first solid food for the baby is rice cereal, an instant cereal designed especially for babies. Initial meals of solid food should be considered practice feedings, and do not count toward that day's total number of feedings. Give the baby one solid-food meal per day, but continue with the normal breastfeeding or formula routine.

[**1**] Prepare the cereal. Mix one tablespoon (15 mL) cereal with three tablespoons (45 mL) breast milk, water, or prepared formula in a bowl or cup. Keep mixing until there are no lumps. The food should have a runny consistency. It can be served cold or warm.

[**2**] Seat the baby on your lap or in a supportive highchair.

[**3**] Place a bib on the baby.

[**4**] Fill half a baby-sized spoon with rice cereal and insert it into the mouth. The baby may push it out with his tongue. This is normal, since all models move their tongues forward and back while sucking. With practice, the baby will discover how to keep the food in his mouth to swallow it.

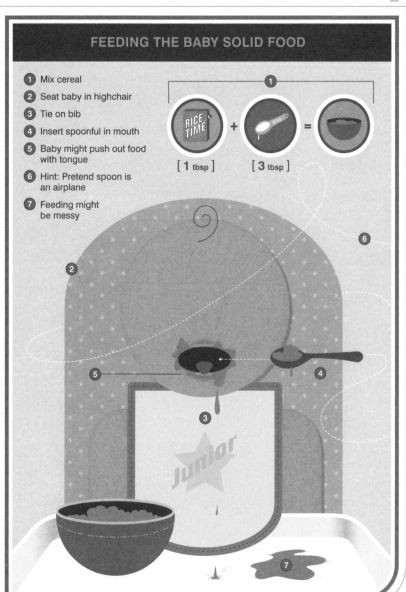

FEEDING THE BABY SOLID FOOD

1. Mix cereal
2. Seat baby in highchair
3. Tie on bib
4. Insert spoonful in mouth
5. Baby might push out food with tongue
6. Hint: Pretend spoon is an airplane
7. Feeding might be messy

[1 tbsp] + [3 tbsp] =

RICE TIME

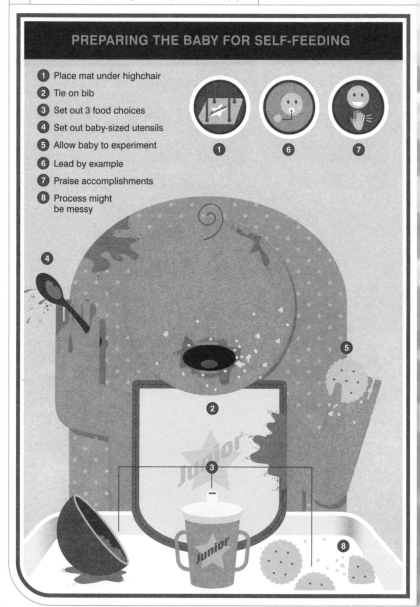

[5] Repeat step 4 with a new spoonful of cereal or with food expelled from the baby's mouth until the cereal is finished or the baby appears to be full.

[6] Be patient. The baby is learning a complicated new skill—one that is very different from sucking. Consult with the baby's service provider about the best time to introduce pureed fruits or vegetables, either fresh or jarred, and any chunky foods.

Preparing the Baby for Self-Feeding

The baby comes pre-installed with a pincer grasp that enables the baby to automatically feed himself. This grasp requires at least 12 months to become fully functional. Practice self-feeding exercises with the baby to prepare him for this independence.

[1] Place a spill mat under the baby's highchair.

[2] Tie a bib around the baby's neck so it lays flat on the baby's chest.

⚠ *EXPERT TIP: Some users undress the baby before a feeding and forgo a bib. The baby is then washed after the meal.*

[3] Set out three food choices. Providing too many choices will confuse the baby. Opt for bite-sized foods—dry cereals, small crackers, and the like—or cut larger foods into small pieces. If the foods have different textures and varying flavors, you will allow the baby to discover his personal preferences.

[4] Set out baby-sized utensils. The baby will not be able to use these tools at first, but he will benefit from becoming familiar with them.

[5] Allow the baby to experiment with the foods. Let him reach for them and try to pick them up. He may not realize they are meant to be placed in his mouth, but most models will ultimately taste any object placed before them.

[6] Lead by example. Show the baby how to eat by picking up a piece of the food yourself. Put it in your mouth, chew it, and swallow it.

[7] Be patient. Do not get frustrated if the baby progresses slowly. This is a very slow process.

[8] Praise the baby's accomplishments. Clap and cheer when the baby picks up a piece of food or places it in his mouth. He may try it again in order to elicit your enthusiastic response.

⚠ *CAUTION: Never force the baby to eat. If you offer food and he refuses, try again in a few minutes. Forcing food may cause the baby to view eating as negative.*

💡 *EXPERT TIP: An indispensable product for any new user is a no-spill cup. This item has a lid and spout out of which liquid cannot escape without suction, so a dropped cup will not spill. Most models will not drink from a no-spill cup until approximately one year of age. Some models are simply not compatible with these cups. The use of no-spill cups will save the user from much worry and cleanup. Follow the manufacturer's instructions for utilizing one.*

Six Foods to Avoid

As the baby consumes more solid foods, he should not be exposed to any of the following substances, which can cause a potentially dangerous allergic reaction.

Honey: This sweet substance can cause a toxin to develop in the baby's intestines. Do not feed the baby honey until at least two years after delivery.

Peanuts and/or Peanut-Derived Products: Peanuts and other peanut products, including peanut butter and peanut oil, can cause the baby to experience a severe allergic reaction. Do not feed the baby any of these products for at least three years after delivery.

Citrus Fruits or Juices: The acid in citrus is too strong for the baby's delicate digestive system. Some models can experience allergic reactions or upset stomachs. Discuss with the baby's service provider the appropriate time to introduce citrus.

Caffeine: Substances containing caffeine or related compounds, such as chocolate, tea, coffee, or soda, will interfere with the baby's absorption of calcium.

Egg Whites: These can be difficult for the baby to digest. Avoid egg whites until the baby's service provider recommends them.

Cow's Milk: Whole cow's milk can cause an allergic reaction in the baby. Stay away from cow's milk until the baby is at least one year old.

Weaning the Baby

Weaning is the process by which a baby permanently switches from breastfeeding to bottle-feeding or drinking from a cup. Do not begin the weaning process during the first six months, which service providers see as the most important time to breastfeed. When the user or baby is ready to wean, take the following steps.

[1] Introduce a cup or bottle of breast milk or formula as an alternate source of food at feeding times.

[2] If the baby has difficulty adjusting to the new source of food, try feeding her in a different location, or change the lighting and music. Create a different mood for the new feedings.

[3] Gradually diminish the number of daily breastfeedings. Eliminate one breastfeeding from the baby's daily routine every two weeks, replacing it with a bottle or solid meal. Consult the baby's service provider to ensure the baby is receiving an adequate supply of nutrients.

[4] When you are down to one breastfeeding session per day, do it before bedtime.

[5] Shorten the bedtime feeding by a few minutes every night.

EXPERT TIP: *Your baby may try to wean herself. Many models automatically detect when the time is right, sometimes after approximately nine months. If your model shows signs of weaning before nine months, ensure that there are no other problems interfering with feeding. It may be that the baby is distracted or uncomfortable, not that she is ready to be weaned. Consult the baby's service provider to eliminate any health concerns. Many models will refuse to breastfeed after six months, but this is often just a temporary strike—the baby will usually resume breastfeeding after a few days.*

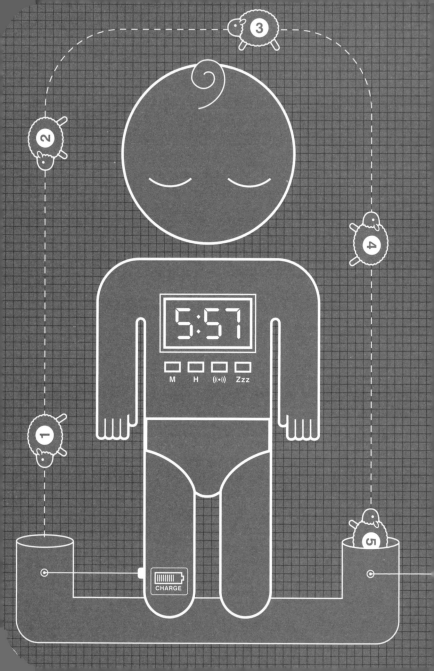

Chapter 4

Programming Sleep Mode

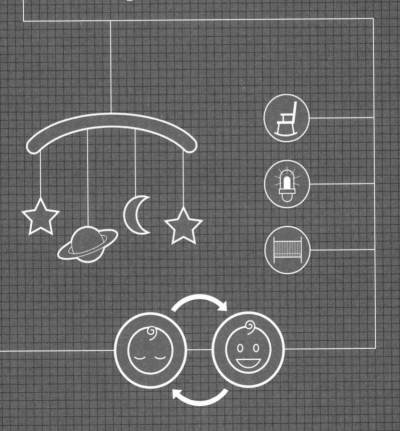

Configuring the Baby's Sleeping Space

The sleeping area is the most important space of the baby's room, and it requires careful configuration. Some users configure their own bedrooms to accommodate the baby.

Wherever the baby sleeps, always position him on his back. This has been shown to greatly reduce the risk of Sudden Infant Death Syndrome (see page 215). After approximately four months, the baby will naturally begin to sleep on his side or belly.

⚠ *CAUTION: When the baby enters sleep mode, remove all pillows, heavy quilts, and stuffed animals from the sleeping space. If slept upon or under, these objects could interfere with the baby's oxygen supply and might result in severe malfunction.*

Bassinet (Fig. A)

A bassinet is a portable bed designed for the first few months after delivery. Bassinets can be purchased at baby-accessory stores or constructed out of baby-safe padding and a solid dresser drawer that has been removed from the dresser. Many users find a bassinet appealing for its portability; the baby and bassinet can be within arm's reach for convenient night feedings.

The ideal bassinet has a firm, well-fitted mattress, with no more than one inch (2.5 cm) of space between the mattress and the sides. Look for solid construction and a sturdy stand that can withstand an accidental bump.

Crib (Fig. B)

A good crib should accommodate the baby until he is old enough to sleep in his own bed. According to current regulations, the ideal crib has strong slats spaced no more than $2^3/_8$ inches (6 cm) apart. The top rail should be at least 26 inches (66 cm) above the lowest point of the mattress. Traditional drop-rail cribs are no longer legally manufactured, sold, or resold by legitimate dealers. All mattress supports and hardware should be sturdy and durable. There should be no more than one inch (2.5 cm) between the mattress and the sides of the crib. Check that your crib meets these and any updated regulations, especially if the crib is a family heirloom.

Crib bumpers can be installed to prevent the baby from banging his head on the slats. If you install crib bumpers, the ties should be short, firmly knotted, and facing the outside of the crib.

⚠ *CAUTION: Once the baby becomes mobile (usually seven to nine months), remove all crib bumpers, or they may be used as footholds if the baby tries to climb out of his crib.*

Your Bed (Fig. C)

Many users opt to sleep with the baby in their bed. This is acceptable if you have a firm mattress; soft mattresses have been linked to Sudden Infant Death Syndrome (see page 215). Before placing the baby in your bed, clear any pillows, heavy quilts, and large blankets from the sleeping area. Provide a light blanket for the baby. The safest configuration has the baby between both parents, who function as guard rails. A body pillow is not a substitute for a second parent; the bed must be clear of such bedding.

⚠ *CAUTION: Do not let the baby fall asleep on a pillow. This could interfere with the baby's oxygen supply and cause severe malfunction.*

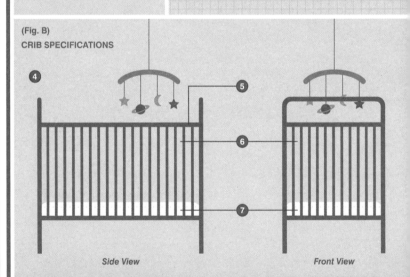

(Fig. A)
BASSINET SPECIFICATIONS

1. **BASSINET**
2. Firm mattress, with less than 1 inch (2.5 cm) of space around it
3. Sturdy stand that can withstand bumps

4. **CRIB**
5. Top rail meets height regulations
6. Slats spaced no more than 2 3/8 inches (6 cm) apar
7. Firm mattress, with less than 1 inch (2.5 cm) of space around it

8. **BED**
9. Owners function as guard rails
10. Light blanket for model
11. No pillows or heavy blankets near model

(Fig. B)
CRIB SPECIFICATIONS

Side View　　　*Front View*

CONFIGURING THE SLEEPING SPACE: Whether the baby sleeps in

(Fig. C)
BED TRAINING THE MODEL

a bassinet, crib, or the user's bed, safety is a priority.

Understanding Sleep Mode

Newborns do not contain an internal clock feature that can distinguish between day and night. Because of their near-constant need for food, most models will sleep in two- or four-hour intervals, often preventing the user from getting much sleep.

These characteristics are not defects of the manufacturer, and they can be overcome with proper maintenance. As a general rule, a newborn baby will require at least 16 hours of sleep every day—but this number fluctuates greatly from model to model. The baby's sleep schedule can be influenced by hunger, growth spurts, and disturbances from within the environment (televisions, electrical storms, etc.).

During the second to sixth months, the baby will need less sleep than required during the first month. By the end of the third month, some models will sleep for six hours straight, sometimes during the night. Other models will not start to sleep for long periods during the night until after one year. The baby's ability to sleep longer might be influenced by where the baby sleeps and what method you use to put the baby to sleep. At this stage in life, all models require a total of 14 to 15 hours of sleep every day.

By seven to twelve months of age, the baby should sleep for long, uninterrupted periods of the night. This evolution continues to occur because the baby needs to eat less frequently and has maturing sleep cycles. As during the second- to sixth-month stage, the duration of the baby's sleep cycle might be influenced by where the baby sleeps and what method you use to put the baby to sleep. The baby will still require 13 to 15 hours of sleep every day.

Understanding Sleep Cycles

During the baby's first few months, sleep cycles follow a distinct pattern. First, the baby will experience Rapid Eye Movement (REM) sleep, then non-REM sleep. After a few months, the baby's sleep system will reverse, and non-REM will precede REM. Familiarize yourself with these cycles so you can understand the baby's sleep patterns.

REM Sleep: As the baby enters sleep mode, she will begin in the REM phase. This is a very light sleep phase. The baby's hands, face, and feet may twitch. She may appear startled. These are all indications that her sleep mode is functioning correctly.

Non-REM Sleep: This sleep pattern involves three separate cycles.

■ Light sleep: Indications include no eye movement, and a "light" feeling when you lift the baby's limbs.

■ Deep sleep: Signs include deep, slow breathing and a "heavier" feeling of the body and limbs. The baby should feel almost completely relaxed.

■ Very deep sleep: Signs include an extremely "heavy" feeling of the body and limbs. The baby may not react if you try to wake her.

Advanced Application: The Sleep Cycle Test

If you have rocked the baby to sleep and want to determine if she can be set down without waking, perform the following tests.

[1] Take one of the baby's arms between your thumb and forefinger.

[2] Gently raise the arm two inches.

[3] Let go.

If the baby's arm falls to her side and she does not stir, deep or very deep sleep mode has been activated, and the baby can be set down without incident. If she stirs, REM or light sleep mode has been activated, and moving the baby may rouse her.

Using a Sleep Chart

Sleep charts can be used to track, alter, and reprogram the baby's sleeping schedule. The sample chart on the next page shows a typical one-week sleeping pattern. It is recommended that you make copies of the blank chart found in the appendix (see page 219) to track your model's habits for the first few months.

[1] When the baby enters sleep mode, mark the start time. It is recommended that the user take this time to sleep as well.

[2] When the baby exits sleep mode, mark the end time.

[3] Fill the space between the two lines with pencil or ink.

This chart allows you to study the baby's sleep habits over one week. Use multiple charts to study his sleeping habits over the course of months. Note if the baby enters sleep mode at the same (or nearly the same) times every day. If the baby's sleep deviates from the established pattern, note any unusual circumstances.

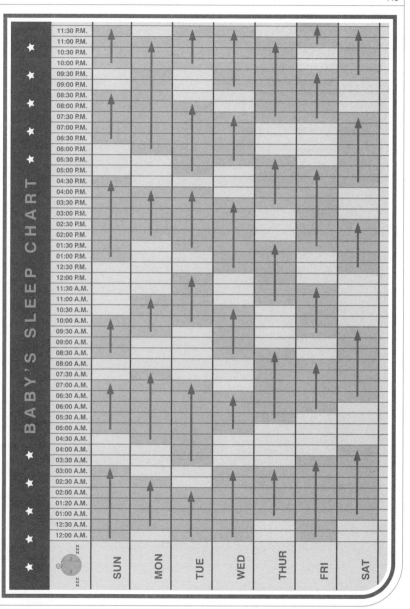

Activating Sleep Mode

The baby might come pre-programmed with cues that indicate he is readying to enter sleep mode. These include rubbing his eyes or pulling at his ears. If you see these signs, quickly work to activate sleep mode. If you do not, the baby may become overstimulated (see page 124) and sleep mode may be delayed indefinitely.

There are two general techniques for activating the baby's sleep mode: User-Activated and Unit-Activated.

User-Activated Sleep Mode

User-Activated Sleep Mode consists of constant stimulation during the day and less activity at night. This approach requires more effort than either version of Unit-Activated Sleep Mode.

[1] Tend to and stimulate the baby throughout the day. Wear the baby in a carrier frequently. Play, sing, and dance with the baby.

[2] Set dependable bedtimes, and keep to the schedule.

[3] Relax the baby before bed. Feed, bathe, rock, or read to the baby.

[4] Condition the baby to sleep using any of the following techniques:
■ Feed the baby to sleep. By allowing the baby to fall asleep after a meal, the baby will begin to recognize feedings as precursors to sleep.
■ Have the non-breastfeeding user put the baby to sleep. The baby's ability to smell the mother's milk may trigger the baby to expect food rather than sleep.
■ Cuddle and rock the baby to sleep. The baby may feel safer in your arms than alone in his crib. Softly cuddle until the baby falls asleep.

[5] Use any of the following techniques to keep the baby asleep at night:

■ Go to the baby at the first sign of waking. Your presence may be comfort enough for the baby to fall back asleep.

■ Swaddle the baby (see page 50). The added security may help him fall back asleep.

■ Place the baby in a mechanical, rocking cradle. The regular motion may help him fall back asleep.

■ Change the baby's sleeping position. He may have been uncomfortable; a new position may encourage him to fall back asleep.

■ Keep one hand on the baby until he falls asleep to provide added warmth and comfort.

■ Feed the baby back to sleep. The milk and the act of feeding may relax the baby, preparing him for sleep.

Unit-Activated Sleep Mode (Version 1.0)

This variation allows for slightly more parental interaction during the night. Begin this process no earlier than the baby's fourth or fifth month. Ensure that the baby's diaper is dry, he is not hungry, and that he is in good health.

[1] Establish a calming bedtime routine to signal to the baby that bedtime is near. It may include a bath, storytelling, or singing.

[2] Bring the baby into his room and lay him in his crib properly.

[3] Tuck him in and say, "Good night."

[4] Turn on the nightlight and turn off the main lights.

[5] Leave the room and close the door. If the baby cries, wait one to five minutes before returning. Many models will soothe themselves to sleep and self-activate sleep mode in that time. If not, proceed to the next step.

[6] Return to the room. Do not pick up the baby. Do not feed him. Comfort him verbally. After a minute, leave.

[7] Repeat steps 5 and 6 but add one to five minutes to the waiting period each time. Eventually, the baby will soothe himself to sleep.

[8] The next night, wait an initial one to five minutes before returning to the baby's room. On the following night, wait an initial five to ten minutes. Continue adding five minutes to the initial waiting period. Within three to seven days, the baby should learn to self-activate sleep mode.

Unit-Activated Sleep Mode (Version 2.0)

This method teaches the baby to self-activate sleep mode independently. Once your unit learns to self-activate sleep mode, he may use this programming more effectively during nighttime wakings. Begin this process no earlier than the baby's fourth month. Ensure that the baby's diaper is dry, he is not hungry, and he is in good health.

[1] Establish a calming bedtime routine to signal to the baby that bedtime is near. It may include a bath, storytelling, singing, and/or rocking.

[2] Bring the baby into his room and lay him in his crib properly.

[3] Tuck him in and say, "Good night."

[4] Turn on the nightlight and turn off the main lights.

[5] Leave the room and close the door; leave a baby monitor turned on so you can hear him. Do not return until morning. The baby might cry for extended periods of time. As long as you have placed him in a properly configured sleeping space, he will be safe. Eventually, he will fall asleep. Over the course of several nights, he will learn that crying does not cause you to enter the room.

Programming a Day Sleeper into a Night Sleeper

Because there is no internal setting on the baby for distinguishing day from night, your model might sleep more during the day than the evening. But with persistence and the following guidelines, any model can be re-programmed from a day sleeper into a night sleeper.

[1] Establish definitive day and night moods. During the day, open the shades, turn on the lights, and make the house active with music and movement. During the night, close the shades, turn the lights down or off, and make the house quiet and calm. The baby will prefer being awake during the day and will adjust his internal settings automatically.

[2] If you must change or redress the baby during the night, do it quickly and quietly. Speak to the baby as little as possible.

[3] If the baby is sleeping for a long period of time in the late afternoon or early evening, change the schedule manually. Wake him for a feeding.

Keep him entertained and awake. He will naturally move this longer sleep period to the nighttime.

Using Sleep Mode Outside the Sleep Space

Use the following guidelines to activate sleep mode when the baby is in a stroller or automobile.

Stroller

[1] Provide warmth. Make sure the baby is dressed appropriately for the weather. Add a blanket if it is cold outside.

[2] Darken the baby's environment. Raise the sun shield, if available. Drape a blanket across the front of the stroller. If the baby cries in response, pull back the blanket on one side.

[3] Navigate the stroller through quiet neighborhoods.

[4] Monitor the baby periodically to see if she has entered sleep mode.

[5] Continue walking or return home. If you return home, take the stroller inside and allow the baby to continue napping there.

Automobile

[1] Strap the baby securely in her car seat.

[2] Pull any baby sunshades down or hang towels from the side windows to block the sun. A sunshade can be purchased at baby-supply stores and affixed to windows with a suction cup.

⚠ *CAUTION: Do not block the driver's view of the road with towels or sunshades.*

[3] Choose your route carefully. Try to drive in a direction that does not expose the baby's eyes to direct sunlight.

[4] Play quiet music.

[5] Observe the baby. Some models are soothed by smooth roads, while others prefer bumpy terrain. Adjust your route accordingly.

Middle of the Night Waking

The baby may awaken in the middle of the night for any number of reasons. All models are pre-programmed with different cries for each problem; the user must learn to interpret the cries (see page 48).

Hunger, wet diapers, and a change in daily schedule are all common reasons for waking in the middle of the night. Rule out these causes first. If you still have difficulty discerning why the baby is awake, consider these possibilities.

Growth Spurt Waking: Most models experience growth spurts (a sudden increase in body mass) at the ages of 10 days, 3 weeks, 6 weeks, 3 months, and 6 months. During these spurts, the baby may be restless at night, and his appetite may increase, especially during the night. These spurts, which can last up to 72 hours, are an essential part of the baby's growth, and there is little the user can do to change them. Feed the baby as necessary, then re-activate sleep mode.

Milestone Waking: Milestone waking usually occurs after the baby has learned a new skill such as sitting up, crawling, or walking. The baby may wake several times a night and want to practice his new abilities.

Health Waking: Symptoms of illness (fever, congestion, and cough) will interfere with the baby's sleep cycle. Other healthy developments, such as teething, can also disrupt the baby's sleep. These are glitches in the baby's functioning that cannot be reset by the user—provide comfort and treat the health issue as best you can. Consult the baby's service provider about administering a one-night dose of antihistamine to put the baby into sleep mode.

Transitional Objects

There are objects that may aid the baby in self-comforting and self-activating sleep mode. Referred to as transitional objects, they can act as surrogate parents in times of stress and will provide comfort for the baby. Transitional objects usually take the form of blankets or small stuffed animals. Many users give the objects names.

⚠ **CAUTION:** *Transitional objects may be suffocation hazards to young babies, and should not be introduced until your model has full control of his rolling-over feature.*

[1] Introduce several transitional objects to the baby during the day.

[2] At night, put all of the objects in the baby's crib. The baby will find one or two objects more desirable than the others; he may sleep closer to one, or will grab at one when you lift him from the crib.

[3] Once the favored transitional object has been identified, present it to the baby during bedtime preparation. He will begin to associate the object with bedtime. The object will signal to the baby that it is time to ready himself for being alone.

⚠ **EXPERT TIP:** *If you use pacifiers to soothe the baby, consider spreading several (up to five) throughout the crib. If the baby awakens in the middle of the night, he may glimpse a pacifier, reach for it, and soothe himself back to sleep.*

[4] Hold the object with the baby during feedings. Allow the object to absorb your scent. Some users place a small amount of breast milk on it.

[5] Once the baby has bonded with a transitional object, purchase one or two back-up models.

[6] Allow the baby to take the object with him during the day. His attachment to the object will deepen, strengthening the baby's sense of security.

Dealing with Overstimulation

If the baby stays awake past the time when he is tired enough to activate sleep mode, he runs the risk of becoming overstimulated. It is difficult for an overstimulated baby to fall asleep. Try the following techniques to activate sleep mode.

[**1**] Avoid overstimulation in the first place. Encourage the baby to enter sleep mode whenever he exhibits signs of fatigue.

[**2**] If the baby has become overstimulated, do not work to entertain him. Do not introduce toys, rattles, or other forms of stimulation.

[**3**] Cradle the baby (see page 42). Put a light blanket over him and your shoulder to darken the baby's environment.

[**4**] Let motion calm the baby. Put him in the stroller for a ride around the block, or put him in the car seat for a drive around the neighborhood (see page 120). Spend 15 minutes with him in a rocking chair.

[**5**] If all else fails, let him cry. Place the baby in a safe location and wait several minutes. The crying may help release excess energy, and the baby may enter sleep mode automatically.

Sleeping Malfunctions

If the baby wakes consistently in the middle of the night and you cannot find the source of the disturbance, the baby might be experiencing a sleep malfunction. However, such malfunctions are rare; consult with the baby's service provider for diagnosis and additional information.

Sleep Apnea: This physiological condition will temporarily constrict the baby's airway during sleep. The baby has a built-in system that will waken her so normal breathing can resume. Symptoms include snoring or noisy breathing during sleep, coughing or choking during sleep, sweating during sleep, and a confused or frightened waking during sleep. The baby might also indicate signs of sleep deprivation (see below).

EXPERT TIP: If the baby is having difficulty breathing while asleep, wake her by stroking a finger across the bottom of her foot. Never shake a baby to stimulate breathing.

Sleep Deprivation: If the baby is waking frequently during the night, she may be sleep deprived. Symptoms include general crankiness and irritability and excessively long naps in cars and strollers during the day. If you believe the baby is sleep deprived, develop a more regular sleep schedule. If this fails, consult the baby's service provider.

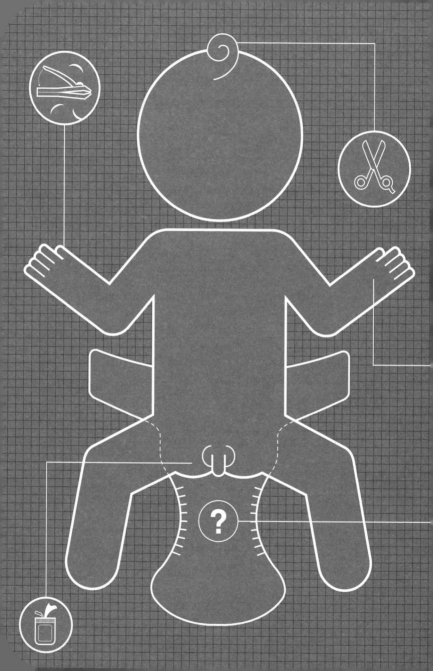

Chapter 5

General Maintenance

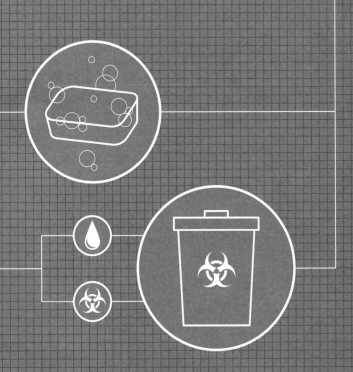

Understanding and Installing Diapers

During the baby's first year of life, you will need to reinstall diapers numerous times a day. Although many users find this process tedious, the benefits far outweigh the inconvenience. The frequent reinstallation of diapers is the most effective way to prevent diaper rash, which can irritate and damage the baby's skin (see page 135).

Establishing and Configuring the Diaper Station

Before installing a diaper, it is important to have all the necessary materials on hand. Experienced users keep these materials in a central household location that is generally referred to as a changing station.

Changing Table: The surface of the changing table should stand a few inches above your waist. Some users purchase this accessory from a manufacturer. Others place a foam changing cushion on a low dresser, a low bookcase, or an ordinary table. Either approach is acceptable—but consider using a table that features storage areas for the supplies listed below.

Diapers: Expect to install at least 300 diapers during the baby's first month, and then plan accordingly. A well-stocked changing station will have at least 12 extra diapers on hand.

Waste Receptacle: Place a medium-sized trash container (with lid) within reach of the changing station. Soiled diapers may be stored there until they are ready to be cleaned or discarded. The receptacle should be lined with a plastic bag and emptied frequently to minimize odor.

⚠️ *EXPERT TIP: If you wash the baby's cloth diapers, do not clean them with any other articles of clothing. Soak the diapers in a hot water cycle in a washing machine, and run the rinse cycle twice. Use baby-safe soap instead of detergents with harsh chemicals. Dryer sheets can also contain harsh chemicals and should be avoided.*

Washing Supplies: A small bowl of warm water and/or half a dozen washcloths or cotton rounds should be adequate. Baby wipes are popular with many users, but they should be avoided during the baby's first month; most wipes contain alcohol, which will dehydrate the baby's skin. After the first month, baby wipes can be used for times when the baby is free of diaper rash.

Barrier Creams, Lotions, and Ointments: These products treat, soothe, and condition the baby's skin. Purchase as needed, and store them near the changing station. Talcum powder is no longer recommended by most service providers to dry affected areas. If the baby inhales large amounts of talcum powder, respiratory problems can result. If you use talc, apply it to your hands—not the baby—and gently rub the baby.

Extra Baby Clothes: Babies are unpredictable and may release their waste during the changing process. This waste may appear in the form of a gushing spray or an explosive projectile. Take precautions—keep an extra set of baby clothes nearby.

Mobile or Toy: These simple props can be used to entertain the baby during a diaper reinstallation.

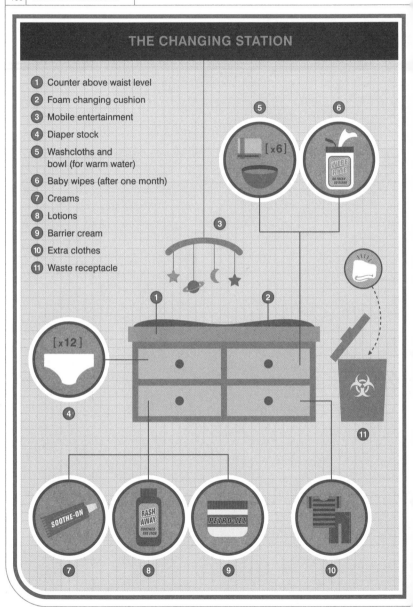

Diaper Bag: The diaper bag should accompany you and the baby on any journey outside the home. It should include a towel or portable changing pad, diapers, extra pins (if you are using cloth diapers), cotton rounds, washcloths or wipes, a Thermos of warm water, barrier cream, a spare set of clothes, and a small toy or two. Replenish its contents regularly.

Blow Dryer (optional): A blow dryer with a no-heat setting can be used to hasten drying of the baby's bottom.

Cloth versus Disposable Diapers

Today's baby owners must choose between cloth diapers (which can be washed and re-used) and disposable diapers (which are used once and then discarded). This decision will have little to no effect on the operation and performance of the baby. Base your decision on your own needs and circumstances, and consider the following benefits:

CLOTH DIAPERS

- feel softer against the baby's skin
- are more affordable than disposable diapers
- do not waste space in landfills

DISPOSABLE DIAPERS

- absorb more of the baby's waste
- can be installed more quickly than cloth diapers
- do not waste water and detergents
- are easily portable

Installing a Diaper

If the baby has an unpleasant odor or begins crying for no apparent reason, her diaper may need to be reinstalled. With practice, the user will begin to ascertain a diaper's status simply by touching it and feeling for additional weight. Alternatively, a finger can be gently inserted to check for wetness. Be sure to have all of the necessary tools assembled before removing the soiled diaper.

⚠ *CAUTION: Never leave the baby unattended on a changing table.*

[1] Lay the baby on the changing table and unfasten the diaper.

[2] Peel away the front of the diaper and assess its contents (Fig. A). If the diaper is only wet, proceed to step 6.

[3] Raise the baby's legs to keep them clean. Grasp both feet with one hand and gently lift them above the baby's stomach.

[4] Using a clean edge of the soiled diaper, wipe the feces from the baby's skin (Fig. B). With males, wipe from back to front. With females, wipe from front to back. (This will minimize the risk of vaginal infection.)

⚠ *EXPERT TIP: Any person reinstalling a diaper risks being sprayed by liquid waste. Placing a washcloth over the baby's penis or vagina will minimize this risk.*

[5] Remove the soiled diaper (Fig. C).

DIAPER INSTALLATION

(Fig. A)
DIAPER REMOVAL

(Fig. B)
FECES REMOVAL

(BOY MODEL)

(GIRL MODEL)

(Fig. C)
DIAPER
DISPOSAL

(Fig. D)
WASHING

(Fig. E)
DRYING

(Fig. F)
DIAPER REINSTALLATION

[6] Clean the area with a cotton round or washcloth dipped in warm water. Rinse and clean the cloth with every pass (Fig. D).

[7] Dry the area by fanning or dabbing with a cotton cloth (Fig. E). A hair dryer set on no heat can speed the process along, but some models may be startled by the noise.

[8] To install a disposable diaper, open the diaper completely and lay it underneath the baby, with the fastening tabs at the rear. Center the baby over the diaper. Stretch the front over the baby's genitals and secure each fastener (Fig. F). Proceed to step 10.

[9] To install a cloth diaper, fold the diaper into a triangle. Lay the baby in the center. Lift up the bottom point. Fold over one side and hold in place as you fold over the other side. Fasten with a covered safety pin.

[10] The diaper should fit snugly—but not tightly—around the baby's waist. Make sure you can insert one or two fingers between the diaper and the belly.

⚠ *CAUTION: If the baby still has her umbilical stump, fold down the front of the diaper about one to two inches before fastening. Do not diaper over the umbilical stump.*

VARIATIONS BY MODEL

MALE

■ Always point a penis downward before fastening a diaper.

■ If the baby has been circumcised, spread barrier cream on any section of the diaper that may make contact with the penis. If the baby is not circumcised, do not pull back the foreskin while cleaning him

FEMALE

■ Never pull back the lips of the vulva to clean.

■ Inspect the sides of the vulva closely for any residue.

Understanding and Treating Diaper Rash

This inflammatory condition can affect any area of the baby that makes contact with a diaper—typically, the buttocks, genitals, lower abdomen, and thighs. The most common variation is *contact diaper rash*, which appears as redness and/or small bumps. Contact diaper rash usually occurs if the baby has spent long periods of time in a wet diaper (moisture makes the skin more susceptible to chafing).

The best treatment for contact diaper rash is preventive. Replace wet diapers often, especially during waking hours, and immediately after a

bowel movement. Minimize the baby's contact with waste materials. When treated with the methods described below, the rash should fade within three to five days. If the rash persists, contact the baby's service provider.

[1] Before installing a new diaper, use a washcloth with warm water to clean your model's genitals and buttocks. The alcohol and lotions in some wipes may aggravate the rash.

[2] Use gentle patting motions when cleaning the area. Excessive wiping can aggravate the rash.

[3] Allow the baby to air dry, or use a hair dryer set on no heat to speed the process. Do not pat dry. Do not install a new diaper if the baby is wet.

[4] If the rash persists, apply a mild ointment to the affected area. Applying barrier cream over the ointment will keep moisture out of the area and prevent the ointment from rubbing off on the diaper.

[5] If the inflamed area has blisters, the baby might have a bacterial rash. Contact the baby's service provider.

[6] If the inflamed area is surrounded by red dots, the baby might have a yeast infection. Contact the baby's service provider.

Tracking the Baby's Waste Function

It is not unusual to develop a keen interest in the baby's waste function. Many owners employ the use of charts to record their model's waste function. This information may be beneficial to the baby's service provider, particularly if the baby ever suffers from diarrhea or constipation.

Bladder Function

Babies vary from model to model, but nearly all will urinate four to fifteen times daily. If the baby wets fewer than four diapers a day, he might be ill or dehydrated. Contact the baby's service provider.

When tracking the baby's bladder function, count each wet diaper as one bladder function, even if it appears the baby urinated two or three times in the same diaper. Place a hash mark (I) in the appropriate box.

The sample chart on the following page shows a typical one-week bladder function pattern. Copy the blank chart in the appendix (see page 224–225) to chart the baby's bladder function.

EXPERT TIP: Many disposable diapers are so absorbent it is difficult to tell if they are wet. Placing a small strip of cotton gauze in the diaper can help you determine if a diaper is actually wet.

Bowel Function

The three main characteristics of the baby's bowel function are frequency, color, and consistency. A healthy baby might exhibit some variation in the following examples.

Baby Bladder Function

Name of Model _____

DAY	DATE	# OF BLADDER FUNCTIONS
SUN	12/21	HHT II
MON	12/22	HHT II
TUE	12/23	HHT IIII
WED	12/24	HHT III
THUR	12/25	HHT IIII
FRI	12/26	HHT III
SAT	12/27	HHT II

Baby Bowel Function

Name of Model _____

DATE	TIME	COLOR	CONSISTENCY	DELIVERY	
12/21	10:15am	yellow	seed-thin	☒ easy	○ difficult
12/21	1:30pm	green	seedy	☒ easy	○ difficult
12/21	3:00pm	tan	thick	○ easy	☒ difficult
12/21	6:00pm	yellow	seedy	☒ easy	○ difficult
12/21	8:00pm	tan	thick	○ easy	☒ difficult
12/22	11:00am	yellow	seedy	☒ easy	○ difficult
12/22	2:00pm	green	thick	○ easy	☒ difficult
				○ easy	○ difficult
				○ easy	○ difficult
				○ easy	○ difficult
				○ easy	○ difficult
				○ easy	○ difficult
				○ easy	○ difficult
				○ easy	○ difficult

Frequency: The baby can pass as many as eight stools per day and as few as one in three days. Breastfed babies usually pass more stools than formula-fed babies because breast milk has a laxative effect.

Color: During her first week, the baby will pass meconium, which is digested amniotic fluid. This greenish-black substance comes pre-installed in the baby's intestines and must be expelled before normal digestion can begin. After the first week, the baby's bowel waste will become greener and will eventually turn mustard yellow (for breastfeeding babies) or tan (for babies feeding on formula). Once the baby begins to eat solid foods, the color of the bowel waste will vary depending on the meal.

Consistency: Meconium tends to be thick and tar-like. A breastfed baby will have slightly runny waste with seed-like pieces throughout. A baby feeding on formula will have slightly stiffer waste, with a consistency like soft butter.

The sample chart on the preceding page shows a typical one-week bowel function pattern. Copy the blank chart in the appendix (see page 224–225) to chart the baby's bladder function.

Cleaning the Baby

To guarantee quality performance, each model should be cleaned after every two or three days of use. If the baby still has her umbilical stump, it is recommended that you clean the baby using a sponge bath. Once the stump has detached, you can advance to a basin wash. When the baby is big enough, baths in the bathtub are warranted.

Before cleaning the baby, make sure the following items are nearby (Fig. A):

- dry towels
- fresh clothing
- new diaper
- washcloths or clean sponges
- small cups or bowls
- hair comb (optional)
- shampoo (optional)

⚠ **EXPERT TIP:** *To ensure the baby's comfort, we recommend that you temporarily raise the temperature of your house to 74 degrees (23°C) during bathtime.*

"Sponge" Bath (Fig. B)

[**1**] Prepare two bowls of lukewarm water—one with soap, one without. Use a soap prepared especially for babies.

[**2**] Position the baby on a towel on a flat surface, or on your lap.

[**3**] Remove the baby's clothes. If your model does not mind being undressed, remove all of her clothes but keep her lower half wrapped in a dry towel. Otherwise, expose each part of the body in turn.

[**4**] Dip a cloth or sponge in soapy water and apply to the baby. Wash one section at a time.

[**5**] Dip a washcloth in the non-soapy water. Rinse the baby with short, gentle strokes.

[**6**] Clean the baby's face. Dip a washcloth in the non-soapy water and pat the baby's face with it. Work from the center out using short, gentle strokes. Wash behind the baby's ears and under any folds in her neck.

(Fig. A)

GATHER SUPPLIES:

1. Dry Towels
2. Fresh Clothing
3. New Diaper
4. Washcloths or Sponges
5. Small Cups or Bowls
6. Hair Comb (Optional)
7. Shampoo (Optional)

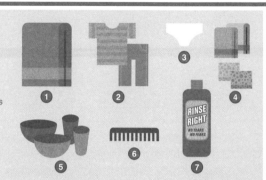

RINSE RIGHT
NO TEARS
NO FEARS

(Fig. B)

SPONGE BATH

23°C 74°F

Lukewarm Water

Lukewarm Water with Soap

(Fig. C)

BASIN BATH

29–35°C 85–95°F

Lukewarm Water

Support Baby's Head

Warm, Wet Washcloth

2–3" (5–7 cm)

SPONGE OR BASIN BATHS: Every 2–3 days for best results.

⚠️ *CAUTION:*

- *Do not wash the umbilical stump.*
- *Avoid wetting a circumcised penis until it has healed.*
- *Do not wash inside the vulva.*

[**7**] Wash the baby's hair (see page 147).

[**8**] Wrap the clean baby in a towel and pat dry.

[**9**] If the baby's umbilical stump is still present, do not wet or clean the area. Check for proper healing. You might want to swab around it with rubbing alcohol. This decreases the risk of infection (see page 212).

[**10**] Re-install a diaper (see page 132) and dress the baby (see page 152).

Basin Bath (Fig. C)

[**1**] Obtain a small tub, basin, or sink, and line it with a pad or towel.

⚠️ *CAUTION: Never leave the baby unattended in a basin. The baby can drown in as little as one to two inches (2.5–5 cm) of water.*

[**2**] Fill the basin two or three inches (5–7 cm) deep with warm water. Use a thermometer to check the temperature—it should be between 85 and 95 degrees Fahrenheit (29–35˚C). If you do not have a thermometer, dip your elbow in the water to gauge the comfort level. If the water is too hot for you, it is too hot for the baby. Adjust and recheck the temperature as necessary.

[**3**] Undress the baby.

[4] Place the baby in the bath. Use your hand to support the baby's head, neck, and shoulders above water.

⚠ *EXPERT TIP: Wet an extra washcloth and lay it across the baby's chest. Pour water on it during the bath. This will keep the baby warm while you wash other parts of her body.*

[5] Wash the baby. Apply baby-safe soap to a washcloth and clean the baby with it. Continue to support the baby's head, neck, and shoulders with one hand as you wash her with the other.

[6] Clean the baby's hair (see page 147).

[7] Rinse the baby. Use a small cup filled with lukewarm water from the faucet to rinse away any soapy residue.

⚠ *CAUTION: If the home water heater malfunctions, water from a faucet may be scalding hot. Never place the baby in the basin before adding water. Always test water before setting the baby into the basin.*

Bathtub Bath

By the sixth month, most models will have outgrown their bath basins and will be ready for a standard adult-sized bathtub. The baby's increased mobility will require slight adjustments to the routine. During this period users should continue to wash the baby two to three times a week.

⚠ **CAUTION:** *Never leave the baby unattended in a bathtub. The baby can drown in as little as one to two inches (2.5–5 cm) of water.*

[1] Install a rubber bathmat in the bathtub to prevent slipping (Fig. A).

[2] Cover the faucet and handles. Use small towels or custom-designed covers from a retail supply store. These covers prevent the baby from turning on the water or accidentally banging her head (Fig. C).

[3] Fill the bathtub with warm water.

[4] Check the water level. Whether you are going in the bath with the baby or kneeling beside the tub, the water level must be below the baby's waist—about two to three inches (5–7 cm) high (Fig. B).

[5] Turn off the hot water first, ensuring the faucet is tight. This prevents burns from a dripping or leaky faucet.

[6] Check the water temperature. The temperature should be between 85 and 95 degrees Fahrenheit (29–35°C). Check it with a thermometer or dip your elbow into the water to gauge the comfort level.

⚠ **EXPERT TIP:** *To prevent accidental scalding, be sure the thermostat on the water heater is set below 120 degrees Fahrenheit (44°C).*

[7] Adjust the water temperature if necessary.

⚠ **EXPERT TIP:** *If the baby seems reluctant to bathe, you might want to join her in the tub. If you are alone, set the baby on the floor mat beside the*

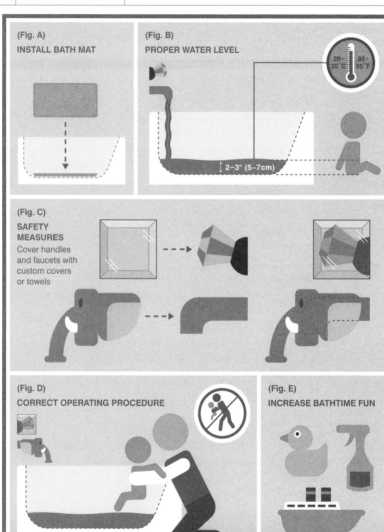

(Fig. A)
INSTALL BATH MAT

(Fig. B)
PROPER WATER LEVEL

29 - 35°C | 85 - 95°F

2–3" (5–7cm)

(Fig. C)
SAFETY MEASURES
Cover handles and faucets with custom covers or towels

(Fig. D)
CORRECT OPERATING PROCEDURE

(Fig. E)
INCREASE BATHTIME FUN

BATHING PROCEDURE: Be safe, be fun, be clean.

tub as you get in, then lift her in with you. Reverse when getting out. If you are aided by another user, have your partner hand you the baby once you're settled in the tub. Hand the baby out to the other user before getting out of the bath. Never get in or out of the tub while holding the baby, as a fall could result in injury, leading to malfunction.

[8] While kneeling, gently sit the baby in the water (Fig. D).

[9] Let the baby spend time playing in the tub before washing. Initially, the baby may be reluctant to enter the tub. Make bathing fun by playing games with squirting, floating, or other bath toys. (Fig. E)

[10] Wash the baby. (See page 143.)

⚠ *CAUTION: Babies—particularly girl models—are susceptible to urinary tract infections if they sit for extended periods in a tub of soapy or shampoo-filled water. Always save washing for the end of the bath.*

Cleaning Hair

Even if your model did not come pre-equipped with hair, it is important to wash her head every three to five days. This minimizes the risk of cradle cap (see page 204). Use a shampoo designed especially for babies.

[1] Moisten the hair or head with fresh, warm water.

[2] Work a very small amount of shampoo (about the size of a pencil eraser) into a light lather on the baby's head. Be particularly gentle as you pass the fontanels (see page 16).

[3] Lean the baby back and rinse. Use a small cup to pour fresh, lukewarm water over the hair. Avoid spilling shampoo into the baby's eyes and ears.

[4] Pat dry with a towel.

Cleaning Ears, Nose, and Nails

Most models will resist additional cleaning after bathing, drying, and dressing. Consequently, many users save these procedures for a later time.

Ears: To clean the ears, use an infant-sized cotton swab to swab away excess wax or dirt on the outside of the ear. Water in or on the baby's ear is not a concern or related to inner ear infection.

⚠ *CAUTION: It is not necessary to clean places you cannot see. Placing cotton swabs (or anything else) inside the ear canal or nasal cavity may lead to malfunction.*

Nose: Use an infant-sized cotton swab—wet with a dab of water, which will soften mucus—to clean inside the baby's nostrils.

Nails: Scissors designed for infants will make this task easier. Cut fingernails as you would your own. Cut toenails straight across. Consider filing rather than cutting fingernails if the baby offers resistance.

💡 *EXPERT TIP: If the baby resists having her nails cut, cut them when the baby is asleep. This minimizes the risk of injury.*

Cleaning and Brushing the Baby's Teeth

Most models' gums will sprout teeth between the fourth and twelfth months. There is no built-in self-cleaning function on the baby; it is the user's responsibility to care for these teeth.

Initially, the user needs only a soft cloth to clean the teeth. As the teeth grow larger and more numerous—when the baby is 10 to 12 months old—users can purchase a toothbrush. Special brushes designed for babies are on the market. Alternatively, users can opt for a standard toothbrush with a small head and soft bristles. Allow the baby to play with it and chew on it before attempting to brush his teeth. This familiarizes the baby with the brush and may help to relieve the pain of teething.

Cleaning

Perform the following cleaning procedure on every tooth twice a day.

[1] Moisten a clean, soft cloth or piece of gauze with warm water.

[2] Pinch an inch of cloth between your thumb and forefinger.

[3] Gently cover the teeth with the cloth. Lower it to the gum line and gently pinch.

[4] Wipe the teeth as you remove the cloth.

[5] Repeat twice for all teeth.

Brushing

Before making the switch from cloth to toothbrush, check with the baby's service provider to ensure that the time is right.

[1] Moisten the bristles with warm water.

[2] Apply half a pea-sized amount of children's fluoride toothpaste to the brush. Most adult toothpaste is not recommended for children under the age of 36 months.

[3] Sit the baby on your lap, facing you, or hold her in front of a mirror.

[4] Place the brush in her mouth and rub the bristles against the teeth. Use light, circular motions. Brushing too hard may damage the baby's gums.

[5] Give the baby a sip of water to rinse her mouth.

⚠ *CAUTION: Always clean the baby's teeth before activating sleep mode. Deposits of milk left on the teeth can lead to tooth decay.*

Shortening the Baby's Hair

During the first year, some users shorten the baby's hair. The first time you shorten the hair, it may not grow back immediately. Do not be alarmed; the baby is not malfunctioning. As the baby ages, hair grows back on a regular basis.

[1] Gather your supplies. You will need an assistant, a towel, a spray bottle with water, baby-safe scissors, and a toy (or similar distraction) (Fig. A).

[2] Sit the baby on the assistant's lap with the baby facing you. Cover the baby from the neck down with a towel (Fig. B).

[3] Dampen the baby's hair. Cover the baby's eyes with your hand, then spray a fine mist of water on his head using the spray bottle.

[4] Distract the baby from the scissors, or he might attempt to grab them, making the cutting process both difficult and dangerous. The assistant should distract the baby with a mirror, balloon, puppetry, or another form of entertainment. Turning a television on may captivate the baby, making him more inclined to sit still.

[5] Hold a section of hair between your index and forefingers and snip with the scissors.

[6] Repeat until all strands are at the desired length.

⚠ **EXPERT TIP:** *If the baby offers resistance, you may not be able to finish the task at that time, so trim the longest, most problematic hair first.*

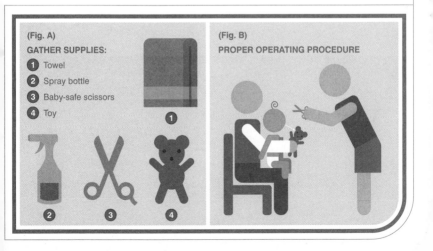

(Fig. A)
GATHER SUPPLIES:
1 Towel
2 Spray bottle
3 Baby-safe scissors
4 Toy

(Fig. B)
PROPER OPERATING PROCEDURE

Dressing the Baby

The use of certain accessories called clothing will protect the baby from direct sunlight, moisture, scratches, dust, and other common hazards. More important, clothing helps the baby regulate her inner thermostat. These accessories may be purchased at any number of specialty retailers.

It is important to avoid dressing the baby too warmly, which may put her at risk for Sudden Infant Death Syndrome (see page 215). It is recommended that you keep the house at a temperature of 68 degrees Fahrenheit (20°C), and that you dress the baby in one more layer than is comfortable for you. (If you feel comfortable in an undershirt, dress the baby in an undershirt and a light button-down shirt.) A blanket counts as an additional layer.

[1] Choose daytime clothing that is easy to remove. Opt for wide-neck openings, stretchy fabrics, loose sleeves, and snaps. Nighttime clothing should be flame retardant and fit more snugly.

[2] Clear a bed or changing station for the baby to lie on. If you have not reinstalled the baby's diaper in the past hour, check to see if it requires changing (see page 132).

[3] The baby may resist being changed. Consider distracting her. Soothing music, mobiles, and puppetry are recommended.

[4] Stretch out neck openings before fitting them over the baby's head. The baby's head may be larger than most neck openings, requiring manual stretching of the clothing. This is not a defect in the baby's design and does not reflect poorly on the current (or future) physical appearance of the model.

[5] Reach through the wrist-end of a sleeve, take the baby's forearm, and gently guide the sleeve over the arm. Repeat with the other arm, and perform similarly for any pants or leg openings.

[6] When closing a zipper, lift the garment away from the body to avoid making contact with the baby's skin.

Protecting the Baby from Heat and Cold

The baby should never be kept for long periods in extreme heat or cold. When transporting a baby outdoors, take the following steps to protect him from the natural elements.

Avoiding Extreme Heat

The best way to avoid overheating is to avoid direct sunlight and over-dressing. Dress the baby in the following items to maximize cooling and minimize the amount of direct sun the baby receives.

Tightly Woven, Loose-Fitting Cotton Clothing in Light Colors: Tight weaves prevent sunlight from passing through the fabric. Loose-fitting cotton garments help the baby regulate her inner thermostat. Light colors help deflect sunlight.

Long-Sleeved Shirts and Long-Legged Pants: Guarding the baby's skin against direct sunlight will help to maintain a lower body temperature. Cover exposed surfaces.

Socks: The skin on feet is particularly susceptible to sunburn, and if the baby is in a stroller, often the feet are more exposed than the rest of the body. Cover them with cotton socks.

Brimmed Hat: This will protect his head, face, and ears.

Sunglasses: These will protect his eyes, which are most sensitive during the first year. Straps that hold sunglasses in place are available commercially. Fit the straps snugly so they do not present a strangulation hazard.

⚠ *CAUTION: Sunscreen should not be used on babies before six months of age, unless proper dress and protection are not available. The chemicals may react with or be absorbed by the baby's more delicate skin. Once the baby is six months old, a small amount should be used whenever the baby is in the sun. Make sure the Sunburn Protection Factor (SPF) rating is 15 or greater and that the lotion is PABA free.*

Avoiding Extreme Cold

The baby should wear one more layer than the user finds comfortable. When bringing the baby into the cold, dress him in the following items:

Warm Hat: This prevents heat from escaping through the head.

Booties and Mittens: These cover the baby's extremities and help keep the baby's core warm.

Winter Coat: This outer layer protects the baby from frozen or unfrozen precipitation.

Blanket: Depending on the severity of the weather, bundling the baby in a blanket can provide additional warmth.

⚠️ *EXPERT TIP: If you plan on traveling by automobile, warm up the vehicle before installing the baby in the car seat. If you will be in the automobile for longer than 15 minutes, unfasten the baby's coat and his inner thermostat will self-regulate.*

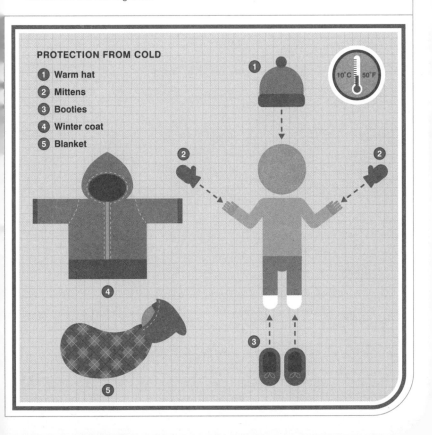

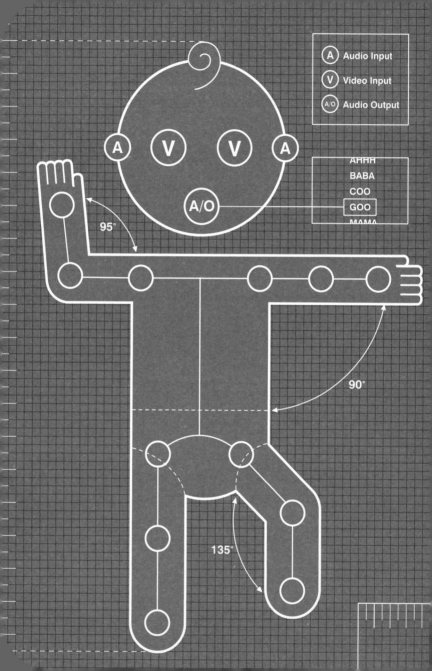

Chapter 6

Growth and Development

MOMMY FINDER

90°

Tracking the Baby's Motor and Sensory Applications

All models develop differently. Following you will find a general guide detailing what many models accomplish by the age of one month, a crucial time in the baby's life. If your model has not reached these milestones by the first month, she most likely will shortly. Watch for lack of development (see page 164).

Visual Sensors (Sight)

By the end of the first month, the baby should have the visual ability to see objects up to 12 inches away. The baby should also be able to "track" objects from side to side.

The baby will prefer to look at faces instead of objects. Most models will prefer black and white objects more than colored objects. These are default preferences and cannot be altered by the user. These settings will naturally change as the baby matures.

Auditory Sensors (Hearing)

By the end of her first month, the baby should have fully matured hearing. She should recognize sounds and turn toward sound in response to familiar voices. Users wishing to enhance their baby's auditory sensors can assist by playing music, talking, or singing. These activities quicken the baby's programmed rate of development.

MOTOR AND SENSORY APPLICATIONS

1. **VISUAL SENSORS (x2)**
2. **AUDITORY SENSORS (x2)**
3. Singing quickens development of auditory sensors
4. **OLFACTORY SENSORS (x2)**
5. Perfume can jam olfactory sensors
6. **PROPULSION APPARATUS (x4)**

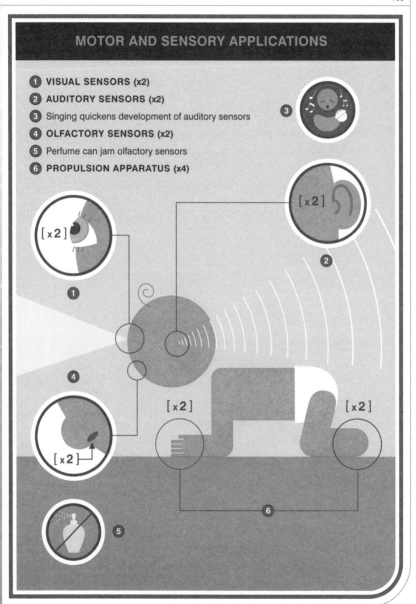

Propulsion Apparatus (Movement)

By the end of the first month, all models should recognize that they have arms, legs, hands, and feet. The baby should be able to clench her hands into fists and bring them to her mouth. She will have some, but not full, head and neck strength. Although the baby can begin to hold her head up, she will still need external support.

Users wishing to enhance the baby's propulsion apparatus should try laying the baby on her belly. This will develop head and neck strength. Playing with the baby's arms and legs will help her realize they are part of her.

Olfactory Sensors (Smell)

By the end of the first month, the baby's olfactory sensors will recognize her mother's scent and the scent of the milk. Users wishing to enhance the baby's olfactory sensors should not wear perfume or cologne or use scented soaps during the baby's first few months of life. The use of such products will interfere with her ability to recognize the user's scent.

EXPERT TIP: Users should not be concerned if the baby has not reached these milestones by the end of her first month. Every model develops at a different rate. However, you should contact the baby's service provider if the baby does not respond to loud sounds, does not move her arms and legs often, or does not track objects or blink when a bright light shines in her eyes.

Testing the Baby's Reflexes

The baby comes pre-installed at birth with multiple reflexes to ensure survival and to accelerate adaptation to the environment. A reflex is an involuntary action resulting from the direct transmission of a stimulus to a muscle. Perform a simple diagnostic test of the baby's pre-installed reflexes, as outlined below.

Sucking Reflex

This reflex helps the baby secure food (in the form of milk or formula) during the first few weeks of life. It usually evolves into purposeful and deliberate sucking by the end of the first month.

[1] Put a clean finger, pacifier, or nipple into the baby's mouth.

[2] The baby should pinch the object between the roof of his mouth and his tongue. He will also move his tongue back and forth across the object, creating suction.

Rooting Reflex

This reflex helps the baby find food. It should evolve into a purposeful turn toward a breast or bottle within the first four months.

[1] Cradle the baby and stroke his cheek. The baby should turn in the direction of the stimulus, his mouth port open and ready to accept food.

[2] Repeat on the baby's other cheek.

Moro Reflex

This reflex causes the baby to throw out his arms and legs and retract these limbs toward his chest. It is triggered by loud noises and/or sudden movements. This reflex expires within four to six months.

[1] Lay the baby on his back. When he is calm (but not asleep), sneeze or cough suddenly.

[2] The baby should immediately react, flinging out his arms and legs and retracting them.

⚠ *CAUTION: Do not make exceptionally loud, frightening noises to test the Moro reflex. Simply monitor the baby's behavior. If a sneeze or cough does not elicit a response, a barking dog, a knock at the door, a raised voice, or another loud sound might.*

Palmar and Plantar Grasp Reflexes

These are tactile reflexes that prompt the baby to grip with his fingers (Palmar grasp) or curl his toes (Plantar grasp). The former evolves to purposeful reaching within six months. The latter fades after one year.

[1] Stroke your finger across the baby's open palm. The baby should close (or attempt to close) his fingers around yours.

[2] Stroke your finger across the baby's foot. The baby should curl (or attempt to curl) his toes.

[3] Repeat with the other hand and foot.

Stepping Reflex

This reflex causes the baby to step down on his own two feet, regardless of whether his legs can support him. Users will have to lend support. Most models will even advance toward the user. The stepping reflex will expire after a few months, and will be replaced by purposeful standing and walking at about one year.

[1] Grip the baby under his armpits, facing you. Use your fingers to keep his head from falling backward.

[2] Sit in a chair and lift the baby into a standing position. Place his feet flat on your thighs.

[3] The baby should press down on his feet as if holding his own weight.

Tonic Neck Reflex

This reflex assists the baby in coordinating head and arm movement. It usually expires by the baby's sixth month.

[1] Lay the baby on his back.

[2] Gently turn the baby's head to the right.

[3] The baby's right arm should extend out from his side. His left arm may bend up toward his head.

[4] Turn the baby's head to the left. His left arm should extend while his right arm bends up.

Defensive Reflexes

These reflexes enable the baby to defend himself against real and imaginary attackers. Defensive reflexes will not expire until the baby has more precise motor control.

[1] Lay the baby on his back.

[2] Hold a toy 12 inches (30 cm) above his head and slowly move it directly toward his face.

[3] The baby should turn his head to one side or the other.

First-Year Milestones

As the baby matures, she will begin to achieve various milestones— but because babies vary from model to model, not every baby will reach specific milestones by specific times.

The milestones listed on the following pages are based on the average among different models. Do not be alarmed if the baby you received does not match these set averages. There is always a range of performance, and deviations from average do not reflect favorably or unfavorably on the baby's abilities. Note that each milestone is independent of others; some models are early walkers but late talkers. If you have genuine concerns about the baby's development, contact the baby's service provider.

3rd Month Development Milestones

By the end of the third month, most models will:

- recognize the sight and voice of their user(s)
- smile in response to seeing or hearing their user(s)
- become interested in more complicated visual patterns
- become interested in strangers' faces
- develop more head control
- sleep in longer blocks of time
- develop more advanced coordination
- tend to reach toward or grab objects more often

WARNING SIGNS: If any of these statements apply to your model after the first 90 days, it is recommended that you contact the baby's service provider.

- The baby crosses her eyes.
- The baby has trouble "tracking" objects with her eyes.
- The baby does not respond to loud sounds or the user's voice.
- The baby does not use (or try to use) her hands.
- The baby has trouble supporting her head.

6th Month Development Milestones

By the end of the sixth month, most models will:

- be able to focus on small objects
- look toward the source of a sound
- repeat and babble simple sounds made by the user
- eat less often and practice eating solid foods
- play alone for long periods of time without crying

- gnaw on objects frequently
- move more independently and learn to roll over and sit up (with some help)
- begin examining the world with their hands

WARNING SIGNS: If any of these statements applies to your model after the first six months, it is recommended that you contact the baby's service provider.

- The baby does not "babble" back to the user.
- The baby does not grasp objects and bring them to her mouth.
- The baby still appears to have active Moro and Tonic Neck reflexes (see pages 162 and 163).

9th Month Development Milestones

By the end of the ninth month, most models will:
- look for toys that have moved out of sight
- become upset when you say good-bye and leave
- try to imitate your words by babbling
- move more independently, learning to crawl and/or pull up
- begin to manipulate and understand how objects work

WARNING SIGNS: If any of these statements applies to your model after the first nine months, it is recommended that you contact the baby's service provider.

- The baby "drags" one side of her body when crawling.
- The baby does not "babble" in response to complex tones.

12th Month Development Milestones

By the end of the 12th month, most models will:

- look for and find objects as you name them
- come find you when you call from another room
- say words (with some clarity) other than "mama" and "dada"
- respond when you say "no"
- move much more independently than ever, learning to walk and climb
- point toward places they want to go

WARNING SIGNS: If any of these statements applies to your model after the first twelve months, it is recommended that you contact the baby's service provider.

- The baby does not articulate any sounds.
- The baby does not imitate any of your gestures.
- The baby cannot stand with help.

Determining the Baby's Percentile

Monitoring the baby's physical development is aided by calculating her percentile. This number describes how your model is growing in relation to national averages of other models of the same age and sex. There are three variables that are compared using percentiles: weight, height (length), and head circumference.

For your model to be in the 20th percentile for weight, for example, is to say that he weighs more than 20 percent of other babies in the country and less than 80 percent of the remaining babies. Note that many models are in different percentiles for different measurements.

[1] Weigh the baby. One way to do this is to weigh yourself, and then weigh yourself holding the baby. Subtract your weight from the total to determine the baby's weight. The service provider will also routinely weigh the baby.

[2] Measure the baby's height (length). Place a sheet of paper on a flat surface and lay the baby on top of it. Mark the paper at the top of her head. Straighten the baby's legs and mark the paper at the base of her feet. Place both marks the same distance from the edge of the paper to ensure that the measurement is accurate. Measure the distance between the two marks to determine the baby's height.

[3] Measure the circumference of the baby's head. Wrap a flexible measuring tape around the largest part of the baby's head, just above the ears. Measure the head in the same place every time.

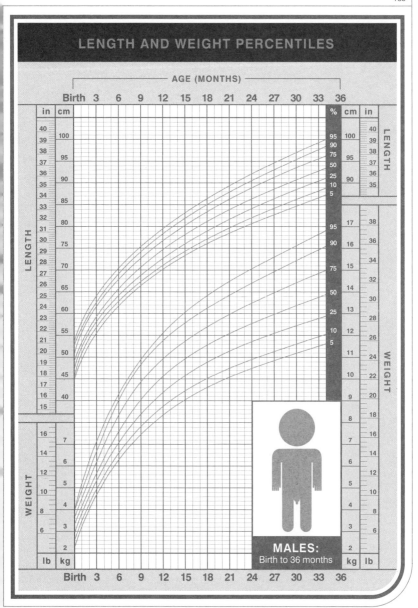

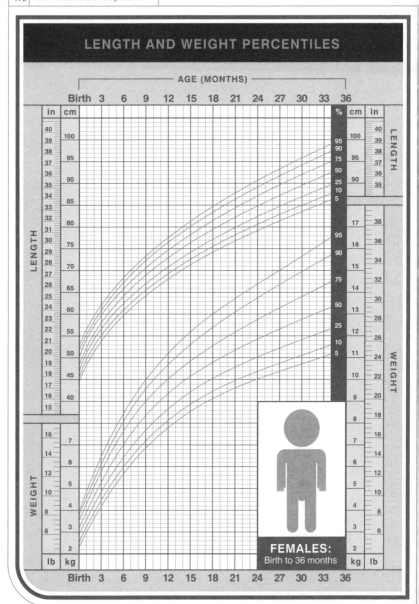

[4] Chart the measurements. Use the graphs on pages 169–170 to determine the baby's percentile and understand how your model compares to other models in operation.

⚠ *EXPERT TIP: Do not worry too much about your baby's percentile. A baby in the 10th percentile for height can grow up to be quite tall. The most important factors in determining a baby's growth pattern are the growth patterns of her parents. People who were small during infancy and childhood may have similarly small children.*

Verbal Communication

By six months, the baby will realize she has a pre-programmed ability to speak in your language. Talking to the baby will activate this realization. Initially, she will learn to repeat sounds you make, and will eventually learn to speak herself.

Some users prefer to speak to the baby in their natural diction and vocabulary. The baby might have difficulty repeating some of the sounds, but she will ultimately learn the correct names of people, places, and things.

Other users choose to speak in "baby talk." This style of communication makes it easier for the baby to repeat your sounds. However, it can lead to future confusion about the correct names of people, places, and things.

It is recommended that users employ a mixture of both techniques. For optimal results, speak in a higher octave. These higher-pitched tones are easier for the baby's auditory sensors to register.

Baby Talk

The baby comes pre-installed with many baby talk expressions, including:

- Coo
- Goo
- Ahhh

When the baby emits one of these sounds, repeat it back to her. This encourages the baby to make certain sounds, and even teaches the basics of conversation.

Natural Speaking

By six months, some models will begin to make sounds resembling fragments of adult words—sounds like "da," "ba," "ma," and "ladl-ladl." To help her expand these sounds into words, employ the following techniques.

[1] Repeat the sound she has made.

[2] Encourage her to imitate you. Applaud or cheer when she repeats a sound you have made.

[3] Respond to sounds the baby makes with natural speech. Respond with, "Really? Is that so?" or "I think you are right." Smiling and showing enthusiasm will encourage the baby to continue the conversation.

EXPERT TIP: While interacting with the baby, many users verbally describe their actions as they perform them. These descriptions can come in the form of statements such as, "I am giving you a bottle now." The baby will appreciate the attention, and might learn more quickly about the uses of language.

The Baby's Mobility

As the baby's motor skills increase, he will develop the ability to crawl, pull up, walk, and even climb. Until he has mastered these skills, it is important to be watchful and to make sure the baby does not injure himself.

Crawling

At around nine months, the baby will usually start to crawl. You might observe him crawling backward, favoring one side over the other, tripping over his hands, or falling when turning. These are normal operations and should not be viewed as malfunctions. Some models will never crawl. This is not a malfunction either—many roll or slide across the floor until they walk. All models will develop some form of pre-walking mobility, however. When the baby practices crawling, follow these guidelines.

[1] Stay within arm's reach of the baby until he becomes proficient in crawling.

[2] Stay on the baby's "weak" side. You might notice the baby favors one side over the other. If so, the baby is more likely to fall onto his weaker side.

[3] Limit the baby's crawling to soft surfaces such as carpets, rugs, or grass. If the baby falls or trips, he will suffer little or no injury.

Pulling Up

Once the baby has mastered crawling, he might begin to pull himself up on furniture, bookshelves, or the user. Until he has mastered pulling up, take the following precautions to prevent accidents and injuries.

[1] Set up a soft fall zone. Keep a pillow or soft blanket handy to place at the baby's feet when he begins to pull up.

[2] Steady the baby with your hands. When the baby begins to pull up, he will fall in unpredictable ways until his balance, coordination, and arm strength have matured.

Climbing

The baby does not have to be an accomplished walker to begin climbing. Crawling and pulling up might eventually lead to climbing stairs, furniture, and other household objects, on or around 12 months of age.

[1] Stay close. While the baby can manage scaling objects, most models do not come with the capability to climb down.

[2] Support the baby as he climbs over objects. The baby might not recognize his built-in center of gravity and might fall forward onto his face when halfway over an object. Support the baby until he recognizes this feature.

[3] Always supervise the baby during stair climbs. A fall on a staircase can be extremely dangerous for the baby. Keep one hand on him at all times, and watch for backward or sideways falling.

EXPERT TIP: Teach the baby to go down stairs, chairs, and the like backward. Manually turn the baby around and help him lower himself. Soon, the baby will develop the skills to do this on his own, but you will still need to monitor the baby.

MOBILITY

1. **CRAWLING**
2. **PULLING UP**
3. **CLIMBING**
4. **WALKING**
5. Shoes can impair upright mobility

Walking

By the time the baby takes his first steps, at or around 12 months of age, he will be much more adept at catching himself (after falling forward) or landing on his bottom (after falling backward). Still, there are protective steps users can take to help him avoid injury.

[1] Let him walk barefoot. Do not rush to add shoes to the baby's wardrobe. Walking barefoot will help him get the feel for walking, and shoes will be awkward at first. Use soft, flexible shoes only when the baby walks outside.

[2] Clear a path for the baby. He will most likely be watching his target destination—you or a favorite toy—rather than his feet.

[3] Beware of sharp or hard furniture edges. These can cause damage to the baby in the event of a fall.

Dealing with Falls

All models are far more durable than many users realize, and inevitable falls will not likely injure the baby. Upon witnessing a fall, follow these guidelines.

[1] Do not panic. The baby can sense fear and panic. The calmer you appear, the better the baby will react to the fall.

[2] Move slowly (if the fall is not severe). If the baby sees a user rushing toward him, he may become frightened.

[3] Comfort him verbally as you approach. Say, "You are okay and will be back on your feet in no time."

[4] Lift the baby if he requires additional consolation.

[5] Inspect the baby for injuries and treat as necessary.

[6] Distract the baby if he continues to cry. A new toy may cause the baby to forget about the fall.

Coping with Separation Anxiety

Once the baby understands who you are and how much she relies on you, she might experience anxiety when you leave. This is known as *separation anxiety*.

This emotion usually appears around the baby's eighth to tenth month. The baby might appear extroverted around the user but introverted with strangers. The baby might cry whenever you are out of sight, even if just for five minutes. The baby might also wake and call for you in the middle of the night.

Separation anxiety will typically peak by the 15th month. Until then, practice the following strategies to help you and the baby manage her new feelings.

[1] Comfort her when she feels anxious.

[2] Ask strangers to speak quietly and to approach the baby slowly.

[3] Introduce a transitional object (see page 122).

[4] Introduce new places slowly. If your model suffers from separation anxiety, this may not be the ideal time to place a baby with a daycare facility. If

you must bring the baby to such a facility, spend the first few days there with her. Then begin leaving for short five- or ten-minute intervals. Always say a simple good-bye to build trust.

Coping with Tantrums

As the baby begins to understand his world, he might become frustrated when trying to communicate what he wants. This frustration often manifests itself in the form of tantrums.

Tantrums usually appear between the baby's 10th and 12th months. He may cry or whine, reach for an object he wants to hold, kick his legs, throw his fists, or flail his arms. In some models, tantrums have been known to persist for several years. Use the following techniques to manage early tantrums.

[1] Throughout the first year, introduce the word "no." The baby might not understand this word until he is one year old. Use it infrequently and only in important statements like, "No, don't touch. That's hot!" or "No, don't eat! That's a bug!" The power of "no" will become useful when the baby has tantrums.

[2] Try to explain as much as possible. All models have built-in functions that will begin to understand your verbal explanation for why he cannot play with a knife or touch a hot stove. These explanations will help him adjust to his boundaries.

[3] Do not reinforce his behavior by reacting emotionally to crying or whining. This will teach the baby that his behavior gets a reaction from you. If the baby's safety is not at stake, do not respond to the cries or whines at all.

[4] Focus on positive reinforcement. Praise the baby when he behaves in an acceptable way. Clap and smile when he puts a toy away on his own.

[5] Be patient. Service providers call this a "phase," and it will pass.

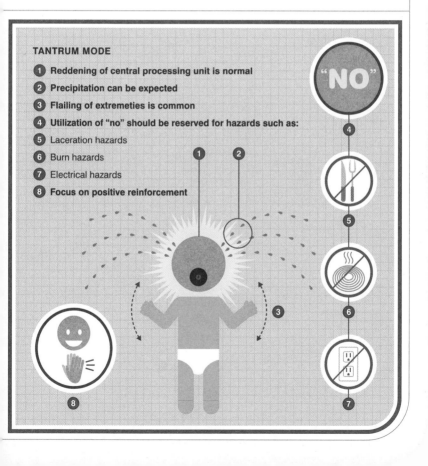

TANTRUM MODE

1. Reddening of central processing unit is normal
2. Precipitation can be expected
3. Flailing of extremeties is common
4. Utilization of "no" should be reserved for hazards such as:
5. Laceration hazards
6. Burn hazards
7. Electrical hazards
8. Focus on positive reinforcement

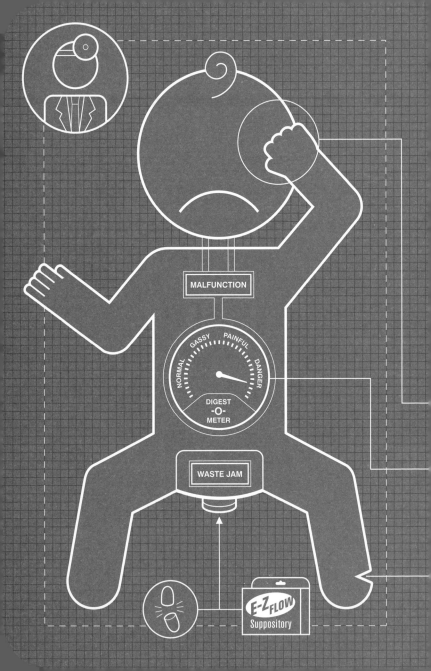

Chapter 7

Safety and Emergency Maintenance

Childproofing the Baby's Environment

As the baby becomes more mobile, at about nine months of age, she is likely to begin exploring her surroundings. Ensure that your model remains safe by childproofing the home. Some users hire a professional service to do this, but users can easily perform this task themselves. Once users understand the basic concepts of childproofing, they can also childproof other homes or rooms that the baby and user may visit.

General Childproofing Strategies

[1] Find any objects that could be ingested or choked on and remove them.

[2] Cover electrical outlets and secure electrical cords. Use safety plugs to restrict access to unused outlets. Use electrical-cord channels to mount dangling lamp cords to the floor or wall.

[3] Install door stops on interior doors. These devices, found in hardware stores, prevent doors from opening or closing all the way. This ensures that the baby's fingers are never closed in the door and she cannot close herself in a room.

[4] Install locks on the windows. If you have crank-operated windows, remove the cranks and store them out of reach.

[5] Secure loose or hanging window shade strings up high. These can be a strangulation hazard.

[6] Install gates across stairways and in the doorways of off-limit rooms. Install pressure-fitted gates only at the bottom of the stairs. Top-of-stair gates should always be fastened securely to the wall.

[7] Secure bookcases and other furniture that can tip over. If the baby attempts to pull herself up by holding one of these objects, she could pull the furniture down onto herself if it is not secure.

[8] Vacuum the floors and carpets frequently. Inhaled dust or dirt can lead to breathing malfunctions, and dirt transferred from the baby's hands to her mouth can make her sick.

[9] Install fire-safety devices. Fire extinguishers, smoke and carbon monoxide detectors, and escape ladders should be fully functioning and easily accessible.

[10] Secure heating vents and cold-air returns. Install plastic shields on heating vents to prevent burns. If the cold-air return is built into the floor, make sure it is sturdy enough to support the weight of the baby. Replace it if necessary.

⚠️ **EXPERT TIP:** *If you live in an old building, or have any loose or chipping paint, test for lead. Remove any chipping paint and all lead-based materials.*

[11] Remove or secure any guns in the home. Lock any firearms in a box, and store ammunition in a separate room.

Kitchen Strategies

When you are cooking or baking, it is recommended that you keep the baby out of the kitchen. Take the following precautions for securing the kitchen.

[1] Put all knives, plastic bags, and sharp kitchen utensils in a locked drawer.

[2] Lock away cleaning supplies, fire extinguishers, and other poison threats in high places.

[3] Secure all appliances. Put a lock on the refrigerator and plastic guards on the stove knobs. Be sure the dishwasher and/or trash compactor lock operates properly. Unplug any appliances that are not in use.

[4] Practice safe cooking. Use the back burners first, and keep all pot handles turned toward the rear of the stove.

[5] Create a baby-safe drawer or cupboard that the baby is allowed to explore. Fill it with wooden spoons, small pots and pans, plastic bowls, and other safe items.

Bathroom Strategies

The bathroom is full of hard and potentially slippery surfaces, and the baby should not be allowed to explore this area alone. For times when the baby joins users in the bathroom, take the following precautions.

[1] Install a toilet seat lock. Get in the habit of closing the toilet seat and lid. The lock will secure both to the bowl.

[2] Lock away toiletries. Put all medicines, lotions, toothpastes, and mouthwashes in a cabinet out of the baby's reach. Lock the cabinet for added security.

[3] Install ground fault circuit interrupt (GFCI) outlets. These outlets will break the circuit, cutting off power, if an outlet becomes wet or overloaded.

[4] Keep bathroom appliances unplugged and stored away.

[5] Avoid placing potentially dangerous objects such as razor blades or empty makeup bottles in the trash can.

[6] Lay a carpet or rug on hard or tiled surfaces.

[7] Make sure the bathtub is safe (see page 144).

Bedroom Strategies

[1] If the baby spends a lot of time in the user's bed, install safety rails to prevent falls.

[2] Secure the area underneath the bed. Remove large boxes that could trap the baby under the bed. Remove small items that could pose a choking hazard.

Living Room Strategies

[1] Secure the fireplace. Install grills to restrict the baby's access. Remove and store any keys or knobs that operate a gas fireplace. Store matches for a wood-burning fireplace out of the baby's reach.

[2] Install padding on sharp corners or on the edges of low-lying tables. Consider trading in a glass, stone, metal, or square table for a circular wooden one.

Dining Room Strategies

[1] Remove tablecloths. If you use one for a dinner or party, remove it immediately after the event. If the baby tugs on it, items resting atop it can fall onto the baby.

[2] Place all alcoholic beverages in a high, locked cabinet.

Travel Strategies

When you travel, it is important to make the new space safe. Give the baby an extra level of supervision until you have secured the area.

Assembling a Baby First-Aid Kit

All users should create a first-aid kit containing tools, patches, and accessories designed to treat the baby in the event of an emergency. Some users will create one kit for the home, another for the car, and a portable kit to use while traveling. The kits should be readily accessible but out of the baby's reach. It is recommended that you check the kit monthly to replace any expired medications or outdated supplies. Purchase a plastic bin for the small items and keep large items nearby.

The first-aid kit should contain:

- Bandages, tape, and pads
- Sterile gauze bandages and strips
- Cotton balls
- Cotton swabs
- Adhesive bandages
- Surgical tape
- Digital thermometer
- Scissors
- Tweezers
- Medicine dropper or dispenser
- Flashlight with extra batteries
- Extra blanket
- Antiseptic cream
- Antibiotic ointment
- Calamine lotion
- Burn spray or ointment
- Hydrocortisone cream (1% or less)
- Petroleum jelly
- Soap
- Bottle of clean water
- Ibuprofen or acetaminophen
- Diphenhydramine or other antihistamine
- Decongestants
- Cough suppressants
- Other medications specific to your model's health
- CPR and Heimlich maneuver instruction card or manual
- Ipecac or poison kit
- List of emergency phone numbers
- Sterile hand wipes

Heimlich Maneuver and Cardio-pulmonary Resuscitation (CPR)

If the baby's airway becomes obstructed by an object, the Heimlich maneuver can be used to remove it. If the baby's breathing has stopped, cardiopulmonary resuscitation, or CPR, will restore it. All primary and secondary caregivers should be familiar with both procedures. Your local health agencies might offer free training.

Identifying Respiratory Problems

[1] Watch for warning signs. Is the baby having difficulty breathing? Is the baby turning blue? Is the baby choking, unconscious, or unresponsive to stimulus?

EXPERT TIP: You can usually listen and/or feel to see if the baby is breathing. If you hold an unbreakable mirror up to the nose and mouth of a baby, the mirror will fog if the baby is breathing.

[2] Instruct someone to call emergency paramedics. If you are alone, proceed with the Heimlich maneuver or CPR for one minute, then call and return to the baby.

[3] Evaluate the problem. Is the baby not breathing? Is she in the middle of a meal? Is an object lodged in her throat? If so, utilize the Heimlich maneuver (see next page).

Is the baby's breathing partially impeded? Can you hear wheezing, gagging, or coughing? If so, sit the baby forward and allow her to try to clear the obstruction through the natural reflexes of coughing and gagging. If choking persists after two to three minutes, seek emergency assistance. Do not perform the Heimlich maneuver in this situation; you risk lodging the object further.

If the baby is unconscious but does not seem to have an obstruction in her airway, perform CPR (see page 191).

If the baby is currently sick, or if the baby has allergies that might affect her ability to breathe, do not perform the Heimlich maneuver or CPR; call emergency paramedics immediately and follow their instructions.

Performing the Heimlich Maneuver

[1] Sit down. Extend one leg out straight.

[2] Hold the baby so she straddles your forearm belly-side down. Support the baby's head and neck with your hand. Support your arm and the baby with your outstretched leg. This will angle the baby so that her head is lower than her body.

[3] With your other hand, perform back blows (Fig. A). Deliver five gentle but firm blows directly between the baby's shoulder blades. If the obstruction falls out, stop performing the procedure. If choking persists, go to the next step.

[4] Turn the baby so she is laying face up along your outstretched leg's thigh, with her head near your knee and turned up to one side. This angles the baby's body so her head is lower than her body. Support her head and neck.

[5] Perform front compressions (Fig. B). Visualize an imaginary horizontal line across the baby's nipples. Place two fingers about half an inch (1.3 cm)

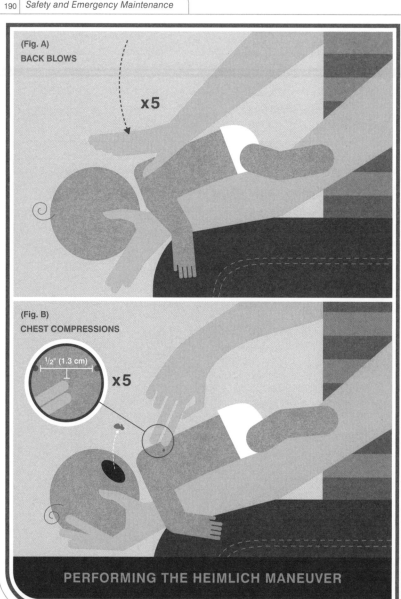

below this imaginary line, on the baby's sternum. Press down gently but firmly five times.

[6] Repeat steps 2 through 5 until the airway is clear.

[7] Check for breathing. Do not insert your finger into the baby's mouth and sweep from side to side—this could force the object back into the throat.

[8] If you cannot clear the airway, continue steps 2 through 7 until paramedics arrive.

Performing Cardiopulmonary Resuscitation (CPR)

[1] Check the baby's pulse using the following procedure (check for no longer than 10 seconds):

■ Bring one arm away from her body and fully extend it to one side, making a 90-degree angle with her body.

■ Place two fingers on the inside of the bicep, between the shoulder and elbow. You should be able to feel a pulse (Fig. A, next page).

[2] If you feel a pulse but the baby is not breathing and you have performed the Heimlich maneuver, go to step 5 and perform mouth-to-mouth resuscitation. If no pulse is found, begin CPR using the sequence compressions, airway, breathing (C-A-B). Begin within 10 seconds.

[3] Visualize an imaginary line across the baby's nipples. Place two fingers about half an inch (1.3 cm) below this imaginary line, just on the baby's sternum.

[4] Compress the chest one half to one inch (1.3–2.5 cm) 30 times in an 18-second span.

[5] Deliver a breath using mouth-to-mouth resuscitation.
- Lift the baby's chin so that her head is tilted slightly backward (Fig. B).
- Place you mouth over the baby's nose and mouth.
- Deliver two brief breaths, one breath every 3 to 5 seconds (Fig. C).

⚠ **CAUTION:** *Use just a mouthful of air. Remember that the baby's lungs are very small. Do not attempt to transfer all of the air in your lungs to the baby's lungs. One mouthful of air will suffice.*

[6] Watch the baby's chest. It should rise and fall as you deliver breaths. If the baby begins to breathe on her own, stop performing CPR.

[7] Check the baby's breathing and pulse. If they have not been restored, repeat steps 4, 5, and 6. If the baby's breathing and pulse are restored, proceed to step 8.

[8] Once the baby is resuscitated, visit the emergency room. The baby should be examined to make sure there are no other injuries.

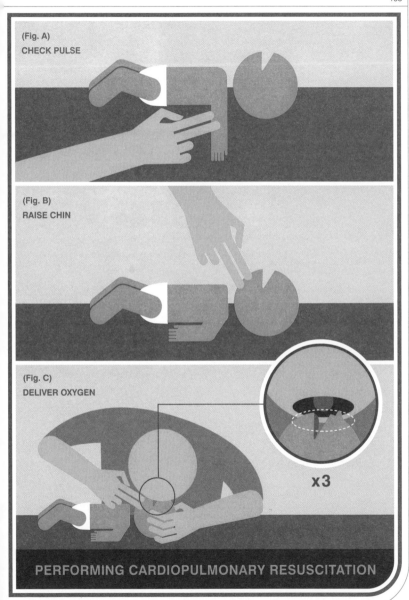

(Fig. A)
CHECK PULSE

(Fig. B)
RAISE CHIN

(Fig. C)
DELIVER OXYGEN

x3

PERFORMING CARDIOPULMONARY RESUSCITATION

Measuring the Baby's Core Temperature

The core temperature of the baby should be approximately 98.6 degrees Fahrenheit (37˚C). This number will fluctuate throughout the day, registering lower in the morning than in the evening.

The easiest and most accurate way to measure the baby's core temperature is by inserting a digital thermometer into the baby's rectum. Traditional glass thermometers may also be used, but they break easily and can cause damage to the baby.

⚠ *CAUTION: Babies lack the patience and motor skills to have their temperature taken orally (Fig. B).*

[1] Prepare the thermometer. Rinse with warm water and dry. Apply a small amount of petroleum jelly or other lubricant to the tip.

[2] Prepare the baby. Lay the baby on a flat surface on his back and remove his clothing and diaper. Alternatively, lay the baby on his belly across your lap.

[3] Insert the thermometer. Spread the baby's buttocks and insert no more than one inch (2.5 cm) of the thermometer (Fig. A).

[4] Hold the thermometer in place for two minutes. Keeping the buttocks held together will minimize discomfort. Most digital thermometers beep to indicate they have finished measuring.

[5] Remove the thermometer. Cover the baby's bottom with a cloth or diaper.

⚠ **CAUTION:** *Rectal thermometers can stimulate the baby's bowels. Place a towel under the baby before taking his temperature.*

[6] Read the baby's temperature. If it is higher than 101 degrees Fahrenheit (38˚C), contact the baby's service provider immediately.

💡 **EXPERT TIP:** *You might want to measure the temperature at the armpit (Fig. B). Be aware that this temperature may register as slightly lower than a temperature recorded at the rectum. Gauge temperature shifts only by comparing measurements taken at the same location.*

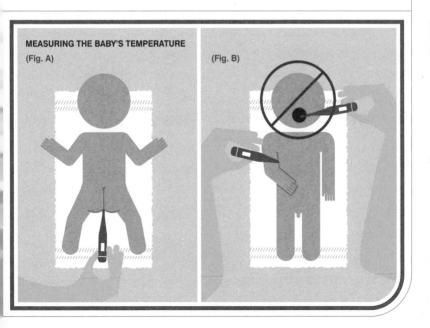

MEASURING THE BABY'S TEMPERATURE
(Fig. A)

(Fig. B)

Medical Maintenance

Most models will experience an average of four illnesses in the first year. It is recommended that users contact the baby's service provider at the first signs of illness. The service provider can diagnose and treat any illness or, if needed, recommend a specialist.

Asthma

Asthma is a condition that affects the baby's bronchial tubes, restricting breathing. An asthma attack can be serious if not treated properly.

Symptoms include coughing (especially at night), wheezing, and fast or labored breathing (your unit will be using auxiliary chest muscles to breathe). The baby's service provider should diagnose and prescribe a course of treatment. The frequency of the attacks might be reduced by limiting the baby's exposure to certain foods, medications, pollutants, temperature shifts, or allergens.

Baby Acne

Baby acne is more unsightly than serious, and typically disappears after six weeks of its appearance. It will assume the form of tiny pimples on the baby's face.

To treat baby acne, wash the baby's face daily, with or without a mild soap and lukewarm water. Keep the baby's bed sheets clean. The baby's service provider can prescribe the use of a mild topical steroid cream.

Birth Marks and Birth Rashes

Birth marks and rashes are alterations in the pigment of the baby's

BIRTH MARKS AND BIRTH RASHES

1 Stork bites
2 Milia
3 Erythema toxicum
4 Café-au-lait spots
5 Mongolian spots

skin. These are not health risks but should be identified in the first few weeks, so you will not confuse them with bruises or localized rashes later. Some markings take weeks to fade away, others take years. If you have any concerns about a mark's significance, discuss it with the baby's service provider. The most common types include the following:

Mongolian Spots: These bluish-green marks, often mistaken for bruises, are typically found on or around a baby's buttocks and/or lower back. Mongolian spots are most common on babies of African, Latino, Native American, and Asian descent, but they can appear on any infant model. The spots will generally fade by the time the baby is two or three years old.

Stork Bites: These pink- or salmon-colored patches, often mistaken for rashes, are typically found on the baby's neck, forehead, nose, or eyebrows. The spots may redden when the baby cries or develops a fever; they generally disappear by the age of six months.

Erythema Toxicum: These yellow-white "blisters," sometimes mistaken for an infection, are surrounded by a red lining. During the baby's first few weeks of life, these marks can spread all over the baby's body—but they usually disappear by the age of three weeks.

Milia: These yellow-white areas will typically appear on the baby's nose. They are caused by gland secretions and usually disappear within three weeks of appearance.

Café-au-Lait Spots: These pale brown patches might appear on the baby's trunk or extremities. If you find more than six of these spots, contact the baby's service provider.

Bumps and Bruises

Bumps and bruises should heal themselves within a week to 10 days. Unless they are accompanied by other symptoms, they are easily treatable at home.

[1] Apply a cold compress to the impact site. Hold a cold washcloth or gel pack on or near the affected area. The cold may diminish the size of the bump or bruise.

[2] Avoid touching the area; it will be tender and sore. Adjust your handling and feeding positions to minimize contact.

[3] Observe the area as it heals. Bumps will grow smaller as they fade. Bruises will change from purple to yellow and then fade.

Chickenpox

Chickenpox is a viral infection that causes a rash. Until all of its sores have scabbed over, chickenpox is highly contagious to anyone who hasn't had it (or been vaccinated against it).

The rash initially appears as red dots and quickly accelerates to blisters and scabs within 24 hours; all sores are usually scabbed over within three to five days. The lesions are extremely itchy and will cause the baby much discomfort. (Many users soothe these lesions with an oatmeal bath—supplies can be purchased at drugstores.) If you believe the baby has chickenpox, contact the baby's service provider and quarantine the baby from other children.

Circumcision

Circumcision is a procedure in which the foreskin of the penis is removed by a service provider or ritual circumciser. This procedure usually takes place in the hospital (one to two days after delivery) or in the home (eight days after delivery, or as religious practice prescribes). In the majority of cases, there is no medical reason to have a baby circumcised. However, a circumcised penis is easier for a young boy to clean, and some studies suggest that circumcision will result in a decreased risk of infection, HIV, and penile cancer.

The circumcision must be tended to properly to avoid infection.

[1] Avoid water. Do not use water to clean a circumcised penis until it has healed completely. Wipe gently with a soft cloth.

[2] Apply petroleum jelly. Spread a liberal amount over the area of the diaper that will make contact with the penis. This will help keep the circumcision dry, and will keep the glans of the penis from sticking to the diaper. Do this every time you reinstall a diaper.

[3] Monitor the penis for bleeding and infection. Do not touch the circumcised area until it has healed. Look for blood or pus. If you suspect an infection, contact the baby's service provider.

Clogged Tear Duct

A blockage in the tear duct can lead to an infection. This condition is not contagious and will usually clear up automatically by the time the baby is nine months old.

Symptoms of clogged tear ducts include a wet or mucous discharge from the eye (often only one eye). If you suspect the baby has a blocked tear duct, wipe the discharge with a soft cloth and warm water and contact the baby's service provider, who might prescribe antibiotic drops.

Colic

Colic is a term used to describe a set of symptoms that causes the baby to feel distressed. The specific causes of colic are unknown, but the condition rarely occurs beyond the baby's second or third month.

Symptoms of colic include frequent waking, inconsolable crying, and gassy discomfort. If you suspect the baby is suffering from colic, contact the baby's service provider, who might prescribe the use of anti-gas drops. You can also consider the following techniques.

[1] Comfort the baby. Take turns with another caregiver, working in 10-minute shifts. Rock, sway, or walk the baby. Any movement may distract her. Consider wearing the baby in a sling, or taking the baby for a drive.

[2] Apply gentle pressure to the baby's abdomen. This can help the baby expel gas. Lay the baby so she is straddling one arm. Alternatively, recline on a chair or sofa and cradle the baby so her belly rests against your ribs.

[3] If you are breastfeeding, eliminate gassy foods such as cabbage, beans, milk, and caffeine.

⚠ **EXPERT TIP:** *Each user has a personal trick for handling colic. Some say baby massage and warm baths are effective; others advocate frequent feedings. The baby's service provider might have some suggestions.*

Congestion

Congestion occurs when the baby's nasal passages are impeded or obstructed by mucus. This is typically the symptom of a cold, allergy, or teething, and should clear up with the associated condition.

[1] If the baby has loose mucus, proceed to step 2. For dry mucus, use saline drops from the baby's service provider to loosen the congestion.
- Place one drop inside each nostril.
- The baby is likely to start crying. Wait for the crying to stop.

[2] You will need a nasal bulb (readily available at drugstores) to remove the mucus from the baby's nostrils.
- Squeeze the bulb.
- Insert the tube into one nostril.
- Release the bulb.
- Withdraw the tube.
- Expel the mucus into a towel or tissue.
- Repeat with the other nostril.

[3] Wipe the baby's nose with a soft cloth or tissue. Apply lotion around the nostrils to prevent chafing.

[4] Bring the baby's car seat inside and strap her into it at bedtime. Sleeping propped up will help her drain the congestion.

Constipation

Constipation is a condition that interferes with the regular output of the baby's waste system. This condition can last for an undetermined amount of time, but is usually not serious if treated properly.

Symptoms of constipation include infrequent or very large stools with a hard consistency, or a long time (five days or more) with no waste output. If you suspect the baby suffers from constipation, contact the baby's service provider. You might also try any of the following techniques.

[1] Measure the baby's temperature (see page 194). The thermometer might stimulate the baby's bowels.

[2] Give the baby a glycerin suppository. These are readily available at most pharmacies. Insert half a suppository into the baby's rectum and re-install a diaper. Results should appear within 30 minutes.

[3] Provide ample fluids. Make sure the baby has enough fluids to keep his stool soft. This usually means three ounces (89 mL) of water daily for every two pounds (900 g) the baby weighs.

[4] Adjust the baby's diet. Reduce or remove foods that can cause constipation, such as bananas, pears, rice, and cereal.

[5] Change the formula. If the baby is formula-fed, change to a low-iron or soy formula until constipation clears.

Cradle Cap

Cradle cap is a skin condition that affects the baby's scalp; it appears in the form of yellow scales on the scalp that occasionally extend to the face. It will usually disappear by the time the baby is three months old.

If you suspect the baby has cradle cap, contact the baby's service provider. The following maintenance routine can also help treat cradle cap.

[1] Apply olive oil to the baby's scalp. Do this prior to shampooing, and be sure to select a cold-pressed oil, which is chemical free. Massage the oil into the scalp for 20 seconds.

[2] Wash the baby's head. Apply a mild, anti-dandruff baby shampoo to the scalp once a day. You might need to wash the hair twice to remove all of the olive oil; use a mild baby shampoo for the second washing.

[3] Brush away loose scales. Use a soft baby hairbrush.

Croup

Croup is a viral condition that affects the baby's voice box. Croup symptoms will be most severe on the first night and will fade after a few days.

Symptoms of croup include a barking cough, a hoarse throat, stridor (a gasping sound made by the baby when she inhales), fever, rapid breathing, poor coloring, and lethargy. If you think the baby has croup, contact the baby's service provider. Changes in temperature often help the symptoms of croup. Hold the baby in a steamed bathroom or allow brief exposure to the night air.

Cuts

Cuts are a break in the skin caused by a sharp object. Cuts generally heal in a week to 10 days. A prolonged healing may be an indication of a secondary infection.

Symptoms of an infected cut include bleeding, redness, swelling, or drainage of pus anywhere near the site of the cut. If you suspect the baby has an infected cut, or if the cut will not stop bleeding, contact the baby's service provider.

[1] Wash the area with mild, soapy water. If it is no longer bleeding, allow the area to air dry and proceed to step 3.

[2] If the cut is bleeding, apply direct pressure. Use a sterile, soft gauze pad. Press the skin together as you gently push down on the cut. Check after a few minutes to determine if the bleeding has stopped.

[3] Apply a small dab of antibiotic ointment to the affected area.

[4] Apply a bandage. Monitor the bandage throughout the day to ensure it does not come off. Loose bandages can present a choking hazard.

[5] Change the bandage daily. Remove the bandage while submerging it under running water or during a bath to loosen the glue and make removal less painful. Repeat all steps until the cut has healed.

Dehydration

Dehydration is caused by an imbalance in the baby's fluid intake and output system—namely, the baby outputs more fluids than he receives. Dehydration will persist until the baby's fluid levels are rebalanced.

Symptoms of mild dehydration include decreased urine output (fewer than three to four wet diapers per day), crying with little or no tears, severe lethargy, weight loss, and chapped lips. If you suspect the baby is dehydrated, increase the baby's intake of simple fluids (water or light formula). If the baby is breastfed, increase the frequency or duration of his feedings. If the baby is bottle-fed, introduce a pediatric electrolyte solution (available commercially). If symptoms persist, contact the baby's service provider.

Diarrhea

Diarrhea is a condition that changes both the consistency and frequency of the baby's waste output. The condition, caused by any number of bacteria or viruses, usually lasts five to seven days.

Symptoms of diarrhea include increased waste output with a liquid-like consistency. The waste might also be more odorous than usual. If you suspect the baby is suffering from diarrhea, or if you notice any blood or mucus in her waste output, contact the baby's service provider.

[1] Use a cotton round and warm water during diaper changes to avoid aggravating the area during the frequent diaper reinstallations.

[2] Provide light meals and increase fluid intake. Breastfeeding mothers should increase the number or duration of feedings to keep the baby hydrated. If the baby is formula bottle-fed, reduce the amount of formula added to the

water by half. Offer the baby a bottle with pediatric electrolyte solution. Once diarrhea has decreased in frequency, slowly reintroduce solids, if any are present already, into the baby's diet.

[3] Watch for signs of dehydration.

[4] Add a dash of yogurt to the baby's meal. The active cultures found in yogurt can help to restore her regular stool.

Drug Allergies

A drug allergy is an allergic reaction to a specific medication. Symptoms of a drug allergy include hives, runny nose, difficult breathing, and a change in skin color. If you think the baby is having an allergic reaction to a drug, immediately contact the baby's service provider, who might change the baby's medication or try to treat the allergy with diphenhydramine.

Ear Infections

Ear infections are the result of a viral or bacterial infection in the middle ear. Mild ear infections can last from three to five days, or can recur for several weeks. If an ear infection lasts for longer than five days, consult the baby's service provider.

Symptoms of an ear infection include inconsolable crying, grabbing at the ear, distress upon changing positions, and fever. If you suspect the baby is suffering from an ear infection, contact the baby's service provider.

Ear infections are sometimes treated with antibiotics. This is the quickest cure for the infection, and will prevent it from spreading and causing more serious problems like meningitis (see page 216). Different antibiotics are compatible with different models, and it is impossible to know in advance what your model will respond to. Several different kinds of antibiotics could be prescribed before a match is found.

To maintain a balance of stomach bacteria, feed the baby yogurt while she is on antibiotics. It is not uncommon for treatment of ear infections to last an entire month.

⚗️ **EXPERT TIP:** *A drop of olive oil can provide short-term relief for the baby. Use an eyedropper to place one drop in each of the baby's ears. Allow the oil to work its way into the canal. This may comfort the baby until her service provider can offer a more permanent solution.*

Fever

Most service providers believe that low-grade fevers are beneficial to the baby, because they slow down viral replication. This keeps the baby from getting sicker. As a result, many service providers do not recommend treating a fever under 100 degrees Fahrenheit (38°C).

⚠️ **CAUTION:** *If your model is less than three months old and has a fever higher than 100 degrees Fahrenheit (38˚C), contact the baby's service provider.*

[1] Feel the baby's forehead—if it is warm to the touch, take her temperature. See guidelines for measuring the baby's temperature on page 194.

[2] If the baby's temperature is between 101 and 103 degrees Fahrenheit (38.5–39.5˚C), contact the baby's service provider. It is recommended that users administer small doses of ibuprofen every four hours until the

fever subsides; discuss this with the baby's service provider.

[3] If the baby's temperature is at or above 103.5 degrees Fahrenheit (40°C), the baby has a high fever and the baby's service provider should be contacted immediately. Sponge her with warm water, which evaporates quickly and cools the baby faster than cold water, and give her small doses of ibuprofen every four hours. If the baby's fever remains at this level, there is good reason to suspect a secondary infection.

Gas

Gas is the result of air bubbles forming within the baby's intestinal tract. This condition often occurs in conjunction with a feeding, and might pass naturally. Symptoms of gas include burping, flatulence, crying, and lifting the knees to the abdomen.

To reduce gas, burp the baby after every feeding. If you are breast-feeding, remove gassy foods such as beans and cabbage from your diet. Perform a gas-release hold on the baby (see page 201). The baby's service provider might prescribe anti-gas drops.

Hiccups

Hiccups are very common in newborn babies, and they stem from a temporary disorder in the baby's diaphragm. Try the following techniques for ending the baby's hiccups.

⚠️ *CAUTION: If the baby has hiccups, do not attempt to end them with adult methods. Do not try to hold the baby's breath. Do not frighten the baby with a loud noise.*

- Blow on the baby's face. This might cause him to inhale quickly and change the movement of his diaphragm.
- Feed the baby. The regular swallowing and breathing might reset the diaphragm.
- Take the baby outside. A sudden burst of cool air might change the rhythm of her breathing.

Insect Bites and Stings

Insect bites or stings are only threatening if the baby develops a severe allergic reaction. Severe allergic reactions include abdominal pain, vomiting, difficulty breathing, or hives (in a place other than the location of the bite); if such a reaction occurs, contact the baby's service provider immediately. A mild reaction such as itchiness at the site of the sting or bite can be treated with a cool compress. Hold it in place for at least 15 minutes, or as long as the baby will allow.

⚠️ *CAUTION: Test the temperature of the compress on your own skin before applying it to the baby. Never apply an ice pack directly to skin; wrap it in a dry towel first.*

Nervous Tremors

Nervous tremors are an involuntary firing of nerves that causes mild muscular shaking (usually in the arms and legs), which may be mistaken for shivering. This is a fairly common condition among newborns; tremors will usually disappear by the time the baby is three to six months old. If the baby appears to suffer from particularly dramatic tremors, you should contact the baby's service provider.

Pink Eye

Pink eye can be caused by an infection or an allergy, and can affect one or both of the baby's eyes. If the pink eye is caused by an infection, it is contagious and users should wash their hands frequently. When treated properly, it should clear up in a few days.

Symptoms of pink eye include a redness of the eyeball(s), redness on the inner part of the eyelid(s), and a green or yellow discharge from the affected area. The baby may attempt to rub her eyes—do not let her. Swaddling the baby will prevent her from reaching her eyes (see page 50). If you suspect the baby is suffering from pink eye, quarantine the baby from other children and contact the baby's service provider.

Reflux

Reflux results from stomach acid rising up the esophagus through the inadequate closure of a valve between the baby's esophagus and stomach. The condition typically appears within the baby's first few weeks, and can last for several months.

Symptoms include the regurgitation of liquids soon after they are ingested, irritability, frequent crying, inconsolable abdominal pain, arching her back, and frequent but shorter feedings. If you suspect the baby is suffering from reflux, contact the baby's service provider, who might prescribe thickening the baby's feedings with rice cereal, placing the baby in an upright position after feeding or while sleeping, and/or a variety of antacid medication.

Teething

The baby comes pre-installed with teeth that will automatically emerge from the gums in the latter half of the baby's first year. This process is known as teething and will cause the baby to feel pain.

Symptoms of teething include excessive drooling, biting on hard objects, night waking, and agitation, and occasionally congestion, a runny nose, diarrhea, or low-grade fever. There is little the user can do to treat teething. Users can manage the baby's discomfort by increasing the baby's number of naps or giving the baby cold, chewable items such as frozen celery or washcloths. The baby's service provider might also recommend small doses of ibuprofen or a topical anesthetic.

Umbilical Cord Stump

Upon delivery of the baby, you will notice an inch or two of umbilical cord protruding from his navel. If the stump is always kept dry and clean, it should scab and fall off in approximately two weeks. Sometimes a stump will become infected—this is a medical emergency. The cord stump provides a direct line to the baby's bloodstream, and an infection would spread rapidly.

Symptoms of an infected umbilical cord stump include redness or swelling around the navel, a pus-like discharge, and fever. If you suspect the baby is suffering from an infected umbilical cord stump, contact the baby's service provider, who may need to hospitalize the baby or prescribe antibiotics.

Vaccination Reactions

The baby may have an allergic or other reaction to the regular vaccination shots service providers administer. Though somewhat seldom, most reactions occur from the DtaP (diphtheria, whooping cough, tetanus) shot. Reactions will appear immediately or soon after the baby receives the shot and are easily treated.

Symptoms of a vaccination reaction to DtaP (and others) include fever, irritability, swelling or redness at the sight of the shot, and anaphylactic shock (a severe reaction including hives and/or distressed or impaired breathing). If you think the baby is suffering from a vaccination reaction—particularly if breathing is troubled—call emergency paramedics immediately. Users can contact the baby's service provider for less severe symptoms.

Relieve the symptoms of a minor vaccination reaction by taking the following steps.

[1] Check with the baby's service provider: He or she may recommend ibuprofen to treat fever and discomfort.

[2] Apply a cold or warm pack to the site of the shot. Some models prefer a warm pack to relieve pain; other models want a cold pack. Try each to determine which is compatible with your model. Test the temperature of the pack before applying it to avoid damaging the baby's skin.

EXPERT TIP: The baby's service provider will schedule regular visits at which vaccinations will be administered (see page 232). These updates generally occur at ages 2, 4, 6, and 12 months. Give the baby an appropriate dosage of ibuprofen half an hour before visiting the service provider and in the following 24 hours to minimize discomfort.

Vomiting

Vomiting is the process by which the baby expels the contents of her stomach through her mouth. It can be related to food intolerance, gastrointestinal disorder, reflux, head injury, meningitis (see page 216), or other concerns. As a result, the duration of the vomiting varies with its associated condition. If the baby is vomiting, contact the baby's service provider, and follow the guidelines for treating a dehydrated baby on page 206.

Protecting the Baby from Sudden Infant Death Syndrome (SIDS)

Sudden Infant Death Syndrome (SIDS) is the unexpected death of an otherwise healthy baby; it is also sometimes referred to as crib death. Although the cause of SIDS is unknown, research institutions such as the American SIDS Institute and the Foundation for the Study of Infant Deaths have established guidelines to reduce the risk of SIDS. To check for the most up-to-date guidelines, consult the baby's service provider. Service providers recommend the following to decrease the risk of SIDS.

- Put the baby to sleep on his back.
- Provide the baby a firm mattress to sleep on.
- Keep the sleeping area free of stuffed animals, pillows, and heavy blankets. Cover the baby up to his abdomen with a light sheet. Keep his arms above the sheet.
- Do not overdress the baby. His room should be a comfortable temperature (between 68 and 72 degrees Fahrenheit [20–22°C]).
- Breastfeed the baby.
- Do not expose the baby to tobacco smoke.
- Ask visitors to wash their hands before handling the baby.
- Keep the baby away from visitors with respiratory infections.
- Place the baby on his belly during waking hours.

⚠ *CAUTION: A baby is most at risk for SIDS during his first and fourth months. The baby also has an increased risk if he is premature, was exposed to unprescribed drugs in utero, or has a sibling who died of SIDS.*

Recognizing Serious Illness

All baby owners should recognize the symptoms for meningitis, pneumonia, seizures, and RSV. If your model begins to exhibit these symptoms, follow the instructions described below and contact the baby's service provider immediately.

⚠️ *EXPERT TIP: Trust your instincts. If you feel that something is seriously wrong with the baby, do not hesitate to call the baby's service provider.*

Meningitis

Meningitis can be either a viral or bacterial infection of the meninges—the covering of the brain and spinal cord. This illness can result in long-term health effects and might hinder neurological development. Fortunately, many forms are treatable and some are completely curable.

Symptoms of meningitis include fever, irritability, lethargy, vomiting, seizure, and/or bulging fontanels (resulting from increased pressure in the brain). If you suspect the baby has meningitis, contact the baby's service provider or go to the hospital immediately.

Pneumonia

Pneumonia is a viral or bacterial infection of the lungs. Pneumonia affects the alveoli—the air sacks of the lungs. The common cold can develop into pneumonia. Most forms are completely curable.

Symptoms of pneumonia include coughing, fever, rapid breathing (more than 30 to 40 breaths a minute), and retraction of the skin between the ribs (it will appear sunken). If you suspect the baby has pneumonia, contact the baby's service provider or go to the hospital immediately.

Seizure

A seizure results when abnormal electrical activity in the brain triggers neuromuscular activity in the body. Seizures can have many different causes, including meningitis, metabolic imbalances, head injuries, congenital abnormalities, and/or fever. The majority of seizures, however, are idiopathic—which means that there are no specific causes.

If the baby is having a seizure, her arms and legs will shake uncontrollably for an extended period of time—between 30 seconds and 10 minutes. During or after the seizure, the baby may vomit, lose control of her bowels and bladder, and experience sleepiness.

To treat a seizure, hold the baby on her side. This will prevent asphyxiation if she vomits. Do not put anything in the baby's mouth—maintain an open airway. Contact the baby's service provider once the seizure has passed.

⚠ *CAUTION: If the seizure lasts more than two minutes—or appears to restrict the baby's breathing—call emergency paramedics immediately.*

RSV

RSV—respiratory syncytial virus—is a viral infection of the lungs that typically affects the airways rather than air sacs. Most models who experience RSV are usually younger than one year old. This infection is contagious to both babies and adults, though the virus is more serious for babies.

Symptoms of RSV include coughing, rapid breathing (more than 30 to 40 breaths per minute), fever, and wheezing. If you think the baby is suffering from RSV, contact the baby's service provider immediately.

[Appendix]

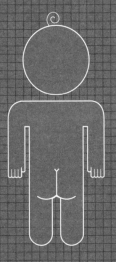

WARRANTY

**No warranty is available for your baby from the manufacturer.
Unlike a vehicle, your baby will appreciate in value after you drive her off the hospital
lot. Every bit of care that you put into your baby is an investment.**

You, the undersigned, agree to:

1. Feed and fill your baby's power supply as required.
2. Change your baby's waste depository as needed.
3. Wash, clean, and detail your baby frequently.
4. Rest your baby as required.
5. Visit your authorized service provider for scheduled maintenance at required intervals.
6. Witness and assist your baby's growth and development schedule as often as possible.
7. Offer love, support, and other general emotionally considerate actions toward your baby.
8. Enjoy your baby.

_____

The Manufacturer(s)/User(s)

Owner's Record

OWNER INFORMATION

○ Mr. ○ Mrs. ○ Ms.	First Name	Initial	Last Name
○ Mr. ○ Mrs. ○ Ms.	First Name	Initial	Last Name

Address (Number and Street)	Apt. #

City	State/Province	Zip/Postal Code

DATE MODEL ARRIVED

☐☐ / ☐☐ / ☐☐☐☐

Day　　　　Month　　　　Year

MODEL NAME

First Name	Middle Name	Last Name

MODEL NUMBERS

Weight	Length	Head Circumference	Apgar Score

NAME OF HOSPITAL WHERE DELIVERED

DOCTOR'S NAME

GENITAL APPARATUS

| HAIR | ◯ Yes | ◯ No | If yes, color | ◯ black | ◯ blond | ◯ brown | ◯ red |

◯ Male   ◯ Female

EYE COLOR   ◯ blue   ◯ brown   ◯ gray   ◯ green   ◯ hazel

OTHER NOTABLE FEATURES

Did you purchase this item yourself, or was it a gift?

Your feelings and feedback upon receipt and inspection of model:

How many other similar products do you have in your house?

Name	Age	Name	Age
Name	Age	Name	Age

QUICK REFERENCE GUIDE

Virtually all current models come pre-installed with the following features and capabilities. If the baby i

THE HEAD

HEAD: May initially appear unusually large or even cone-shaped, depending on model and delivery option. A cone-shaped head will become more rounded after four to eight weeks.

CIRCUMFERENCE: The average head circumference of all models is 13.8 inches (35 cm). Any measurement between 12.9 and 14.7 inches (32–37 cm) is considered normal.

HAIR: Not available upon delivery with every model. Color may vary.

FONTANELS (ANTERIOR AND POSTERIOR): Also known as "soft spots." Fontanels are two gaps in the baby's skull where the bones have not grown together. Never apply pressure to the fontanels. They should seal completely by the end of the first year (or soon after).

EYES: Most Caucasian models are delivered with blue or gray eyes, while African and Asian models are usually delivered with brown eyes. Be aware that the pigmentation of the iris may change several times during the first few months. The baby will automatically settle on an eye color by the age of nine to twelve months.

NECK: Upon arrival, this feature may appear "useless." This is not a defect. The neck will become more useful in two to four months.

missing one or more of the functions described herein, contact the baby's service provider immediately.

THE BODY

SKIN: The baby's skin may be exceptionally sensitive to the chemicals found in new (unwashed) garments. The skin may react poorly to the chemicals in ordinary laundry detergent. Consider switching to a fragrance-free, chemical-free detergent for all of the laundry in the household.

UMBILICAL STUMP: This appendage will become scabbed and, after several weeks, will fall off. It must be kept clean and dry to avoid infection and to form a healthy navel.

RECTUM: This is the site of the baby's solid waste output. A thermometer placed in this port will measure the baby's core temperature, which should be approximately 98.6 degrees Fahrenheit (37°C).

GENITALS: It is normal for the baby's genitals to appear slightly enlarged. This has no relation to the future size or shape of the baby's genitals.

FUZZ: Many models come pre-installed with lanugo, a downy coating of hair on the shoulders or back. This coating will disappear within a few weeks.

WEIGHT: The average model weighs 7.5 pounds (3.4 kg) on delivery. The majority weigh between 5.5 and 10 pounds (2.5–4.5 kg).

LENGTH: The average model is 20 inches (51 cm) long on delivery. The majority are between 18 and 22 inches (45–56 cm) long.

Baby Bladder Function

DAY	MONTH	DATE	# OF BLADDER FUNCTIONS
SUN			
MON			
TUE			
WED			
THUR			
FRI			
SAT			
SUN			
MON			
TUE			
WED			
THUR			
FRI			
SAT			
SUN			
MON			
TUE			
WED			
THUR			
FRI			
SAT			

DAY	MONTH	DATE	# OF BLADDER FUNCTIONS
SUN			
MON			
TUE			
WED			
THUR			
FRI			
SAT			
SUN			
MON			
TUE			
WED			
THUR			
FRI			
SAT			
SUN			
MON			
TUE			
WED			
THUR			
FRI			
SAT			

Baby Bowel Function

DATE	TIME	COLOR	CONSISTENCY	DELIVERY
				◯ easy ◯ difficult
				◯ easy ◯ difficult
				◯ easy ◯ difficult
				◯ easy ◯ difficult
				◯ easy ◯ difficult
				◯ easy ◯ difficult
				◯ easy ◯ difficult
				◯ easy ◯ difficult
				◯ easy ◯ difficult
				◯ easy ◯ difficult
				◯ easy ◯ difficult
				◯ easy ◯ difficult
				◯ easy ◯ difficult
				◯ easy ◯ difficult
				◯ easy ◯ difficult
				◯ easy ◯ difficult
				◯ easy ◯ difficult
				◯ easy ◯ difficult
				◯ easy ◯ difficult
				◯ easy ◯ difficult
				◯ easy ◯ difficult
				◯ easy ◯ difficult

DATE	TIME	COLOR	CONSISTENCY	DELIVERY
				○ easy ○ difficult
				○ easy ○ difficult
				○ easy ○ difficult
				○ easy ○ difficult
				○ easy ○ difficult
				○ easy ○ difficult
				○ easy ○ difficult
				○ easy ○ difficult
				○ easy ○ difficult
				○ easy ○ difficult
				○ easy ○ difficult
				○ easy ○ difficult
				○ easy ○ difficult
				○ easy ○ difficult
				○ easy ○ difficult
				○ easy ○ difficult
				○ easy ○ difficult
				○ easy ○ difficult
				○ easy ○ difficult
				○ easy ○ difficult

Feeding Record

DATE	TIME STARTED	SIDE STARTED ON	MINUTES AT BREAST
		○ LEFT ○ RIGHT	LEFT: _____ RIGHT: _____
		○ LEFT ○ RIGHT	LEFT: _____ RIGHT: _____
		○ LEFT ○ RIGHT	LEFT: _____ RIGHT: _____
		○ LEFT ○ RIGHT	LEFT: _____ RIGHT: _____
		○ LEFT ○ RIGHT	LEFT: _____ RIGHT: _____
		○ LEFT ○ RIGHT	LEFT: _____ RIGHT: _____
		○ LEFT ○ RIGHT	LEFT: _____ RIGHT: _____
		○ LEFT ○ RIGHT	LEFT: _____ RIGHT: _____
		○ LEFT ○ RIGHT	LEFT: _____ RIGHT: _____
		○ LEFT ○ RIGHT	LEFT: _____ RIGHT: _____
		○ LEFT ○ RIGHT	LEFT: _____ RIGHT: _____
		○ LEFT ○ RIGHT	LEFT: _____ RIGHT: _____
		○ LEFT ○ RIGHT	LEFT: _____ RIGHT: _____
		○ LEFT ○ RIGHT	LEFT: _____ RIGHT: _____
		○ LEFT ○ RIGHT	LEFT: _____ RIGHT: _____
		○ LEFT ○ RIGHT	LEFT: _____ RIGHT: _____
		○ LEFT ○ RIGHT	LEFT: _____ RIGHT: _____
		○ LEFT ○ RIGHT	LEFT: _____ RIGHT: _____
		○ LEFT ○ RIGHT	LEFT: _____ RIGHT: _____
		○ LEFT ○ RIGHT	LEFT: _____ RIGHT: _____
		○ LEFT ○ RIGHT	LEFT: _____ RIGHT: _____

DATE	TIME STARTED	SIDE STARTED ON	MINUTES AT BREAST
		○ LEFT ○ RIGHT	LEFT: _____ RIGHT: _____
		○ LEFT ○ RIGHT	LEFT: _____ RIGHT: _____
		○ LEFT ○ RIGHT	LEFT: _____ RIGHT: _____
		○ LEFT ○ RIGHT	LEFT: _____ RIGHT: _____
		○ LEFT ○ RIGHT	LEFT: _____ RIGHT: _____
		○ LEFT ○ RIGHT	LEFT: _____ RIGHT: _____
		○ LEFT ○ RIGHT	LEFT: _____ RIGHT: _____
		○ LEFT ○ RIGHT	LEFT: _____ RIGHT: _____
		○ LEFT ○ RIGHT	LEFT: _____ RIGHT: _____
		○ LEFT ○ RIGHT	LEFT: _____ RIGHT: _____
		○ LEFT ○ RIGHT	LEFT: _____ RIGHT: _____
		○ LEFT ○ RIGHT	LEFT: _____ RIGHT: _____
		○ LEFT ○ RIGHT	LEFT: _____ RIGHT: _____
		○ LEFT ○ RIGHT	LEFT: _____ RIGHT: _____
		○ LEFT ○ RIGHT	LEFT: _____ RIGHT: _____
		○ LEFT ○ RIGHT	LEFT: _____ RIGHT: _____
		○ LEFT ○ RIGHT	LEFT: _____ RIGHT: _____
		○ LEFT ○ RIGHT	LEFT: _____ RIGHT: _____
		○ LEFT ○ RIGHT	LEFT: _____ RIGHT: _____
		○ LEFT ○ RIGHT	LEFT: _____ RIGHT: _____

BABY'S SLEEP CHART

zzz	SUN	MON	TUE	WED	THU	FRI	SAT	SUN	MON	TUE	WED	THU	FRI	SAT
12:00 A.M.														
12:30 A.M.														
01:00 A.M.														
01:30 A.M.														
02:00 A.M.														
02:30 A.M.														
03:00 A.M.														
03:30 A.M.														
04:00 A.M.														
04:30 A.M.														
05:00 A.M.														
05:30 A.M.														
06:00 A.M.														
06:30 A.M.														
07:00 A.M.														
07:30 A.M.														
08:00 A.M.														
08:30 A.M.														
09:00 A.M.														
09:30 A.M.														
10:00 A.M.														
10:30 A.M.														
11:00 A.M.														
11:30 A.M.														
12:00 P.M.														
12:30 P.M.														
01:00 P.M.														
01:30 P.M.														
02:00 P.M.														
02:30 P.M.														
03:00 P.M.														
03:30 P.M.														
04:00 P.M.														
04:30 P.M.														
05:00 P.M.														
05:30 P.M.														
06:00 P.M.														
06:30 P.M.														
07:00 P.M.														
07:30 P.M.														
08:00 P.M.														
08:30 P.M.														
09:00 P.M.														
09:30 P.M.														
10:00 P.M.														
10:30 P.M.														
11:00 P.M.														
11:30 P.M.														

	SUN	MON	TUE	WED	THU	FRI	SAT	SUN	MON	TUE	WED	THU	FRI	SAT	
11:30 P.M.															
11:00 P.M.															
10:30 P.M.															★
10:00 P.M.															
09:30 P.M.															★
09:00 P.M.															
08:30 P.M.															★
08:00 P.M.															
07:30 P.M.															★
07:00 P.M.															
06:30 P.M.															★
06:00 P.M.															
05:30 P.M.															★
05:00 P.M.															
04:30 P.M.															★
04:00 P.M.															
03:30 P.M.															★
03:00 P.M.															
02:30 P.M.															★
02:00 P.M.															
01:30 P.M.															★
01:00 P.M.															
12:30 P.M.															★
12:00 P.M.															
11:30 A.M.															★
11:00 A.M.															
10:30 A.M.															★
10:00 A.M.															
09:30 A.M.															★
09:00 A.M.															
08:30 A.M.															★
08:00 A.M.															
07:30 A.M.															★
07:00 A.M.															
06:30 A.M.															★
06:00 A.M.															
05:30 A.M.															★
05:00 A.M.															
04:30 A.M.															★
04:00 A.M.															
03:30 A.M.															★
03:00 A.M.															
02:30 A.M.															★
02:00 A.M.															
01:30 A.M.															★
01:00 A.M.															
12:30 A.M.															★
12:00 A.M.															

Scheduled Maintenance

To ensure your unit operates at peak efficiency in all areas, recommended service checkups should be performed. The following service interval checklists describe recommended maintenance and updates for a baby functioning under normal or average operating conditions. Variations in your baby's health and/or your own lifestyle may require a different maintenance schedule, which will be recommended by your service provider.

With regards to immunizations and other updates to your baby's immune system, schedules may vary from the intervals listed below. Some updates may be installed over a different period. Consult your service provider for a schedule that best suits the requirements of your baby.

Charts follow for newborn, 3–5 days, 2 months, 4 months, 6 months, 9 months, and 12 months scheduled maintenance.

Well-child scheduled maintenance should continue to be performed by your service provider at 15, 18, 24, 48, and 60 months. Immunization schedules should be continued based on previous service installations and will be recommended by your service provider based on installation history.

⚠️ *EXPERT TIP: Numerous reputable studies have found no link between MMR and autism, and an original study from England in 1998 suggesting such a link has since been discredited. An official schedule of immunizations may be found at www.cdc.gov/vaccines, which takes into account all new vaccines and evidence regarding immunizations.*

Interval: Newborn

HOURS OF OPERATION: 0–1

Year _____

Make _____

Model _____

❑ History – N/A
❑ Measurements
      ❑ Length ____
      ❑ Height _____
      ❑ Weight ____
      ❑ Head Circumference _____
      ❑ Blood Pressure ____/_____
❑ Sensory Screening
      ❑ Vision/Optical Sensors (Pass/Fail)
      ❑ Hearing/Audio Sensors (Pass/Fail)
❑ Developmental Screening (Pass/Fail)
❑ Physical Examination
❑ Fluid Checks
      ❑ Blood Test
❑ Immunizations
      ❑ Hepatitis B (HepB) – first dose
❑ Notes _____

Scheduled Maintenance Performed by _____

Interval: 3–5 Days

HOURS OF OPERATION: 72–120

Year _____

Make _____

Model _____

❑ **History**

❑ **Measurements**

       ❑ **Length** _____

       ❑ **Height** _____

       ❑ **Weight** _____

       ❑ **Head Circumference** _____

       ❑ **Blood Pressure (optional)** _____/_____

❑ **Sensory Screening**

       ❑ **Vision/Optical Sensors (Pass/Fail)**

       ❑ **Hearing/Audio Sensors (Pass/Fail)**

❑ **Developmental Screening (Pass/Fail)**

❑ **Physical Examination**

❑ **Fluid Checks**

❑ **Immunizations – N/A**

❑ **Notes** _____

Scheduled Maintenance Performed by _____

Interval: 2 Months

HOURS OF OPERATION: 1,440

Year _____

Make _____

Model _____

❑ History
❑ Measurements
      ❑ Length _____
      ❑ Height _____
      ❑ Weight _____
      ❑ Head Circumference _____
      ❑ Blood Pressure (optional) _____/_____
❑ Sensory Screening
      ❑ Vision/Optical Sensors (Pass/Fail)
      ❑ Hearing/Audio Sensors (Pass/Fail)
❑ Developmental Screening (Pass/Fail)
❑ Physical Examination
❑ Fluid Checks
❑ Immunizations
      ❑ Hepatitis B (HepB) – second dose
      ❑ Rotavirus (RV) – first dose
      ❑ Diphtheria, Tetanus, Pertussis (DTaP) – first dose
      ❑ Haemophilus Influenzae, Type b (Hib) – first dose
      ❑ Pneumococcal (PCV) – first dose
      ❑ Inactivated Poliovirus (IPV) – first dose
❑ Notes _____

Scheduled Maintenance Performed by _____

Interval: 4 Months

HOURS OF OPERATION: 2,880

Year _____

Make _____

Model _____

❑ **History**

❑ **Measurements**

    ❑ **Length** _____

    ❑ **Height** _____

    ❑ **Weight** _____

    ❑ **Head Circumference** _____

    ❑ **Blood Pressure (optional)** _____/_____

❑ **Sensory Screening**

    ❑ **Vision/Optical Sensors (Pass/Fail)**

    ❑ **Hearing/Audio Sensors (Pass/Fail)**

❑ **Developmental Screening (Pass/Fail)**

❑ **Physical Examination**

❑ **Fluid Checks**

❑ **Immunizations**

    ❑ **Rotavirus (RV) – second dose**

    ❑ **Diphtheria, Tetanus, Pertussis (DTaP) – second dose**

    ❑ **Haemophilus Influenzae, Type b (Hib) – second dose**

    ❑ **Pneumococcal (PCV) – second dose**

    ❑ **Inactivated Poliovirus (IPV) – second dose**

❑ **Notes** _____

Scheduled Maintenance Performed by _____

Interval: 6 Months

HOURS OF OPERATION: 4,320

Year _____

Make _____

Model _____

❏ History
❏ Measurements
      ❏ Length ____
      ❏ Height _____
      ❏ Weight ____
      ❏ Head Circumference _____
      ❏ Blood Pressure (optional) ____/_____
❏ Sensory Screening
      ❏ Vision/Optical Sensors (Pass/Fail)
      ❏ Hearing/Audio Sensors (Pass/Fail)
❏ Developmental Screening (Pass/Fail)
❏ Physical Examination
❏ Fluid Checks
      ❏ Blood Test
      ❏ Lead Screening
❏ Immunizations
      ❏ Hepatitis B (HepB) – third dose
      ❏ Rotavirus (RV) – third dose
      ❏ Diphtheria, Tetanus, Pertussis (DTaP) – third dose
      ❏ Haemophilus Influenzae, Type b (Hib) – third dose
      ❏ Pneumococcal (PCV) – third dose
      ❏ Influenza – seasonal, yearly, various installation options available (consult with service provider)
❏ Oral Examination
❏ Notes _____

Scheduled Maintenance Performed by _____

Interval: 9 Months

HOURS OF OPERATION: 6,480

Year _____

Make _____

Model _____

❑ **History**
❑ **Measurements**
       ❑ **Length** _____
       ❑ **Height** _____
       ❑ **Weight** _____
       ❑ **Head Circumference** _____
       ❑ **Blood Pressure (optional)** _____/_____
❑ **Sensory Screening**
       ❑ **Vision/Optical Sensors (Pass/Fail)**
       ❑ **Hearing/Audio Sensors (Pass/Fail)**
❑ **Developmental Screening (Pass/Fail)**
❑ **Physical Examination**
❑ **Fluid Checks**
❑ **Immunizations – none if previous maintenance schedules are current**
❑ **Oral Examination**
❑ **Notes** _____

Scheduled Maintenance Performed by _____

Interval: 12 Months

HOURS OF OPERATION: 8,640

Year _____

Make _____

Model _____

❏ **History**
❏ **Measurements**
       ❏ **Length** _____
       ❏ **Height** _____
       ❏ **Weight** _____
       ❏ **Head Circumference** _____
       ❏ **Blood Pressure (optional)** _____/_____
❏ **Sensory Screening**
       ❏ **Vision/Optical Sensors (Pass/Fail)**
       ❏ **Hearing/Audio Sensors (Pass/Fail)**
❏ **Developmental Screening (Pass/Fail)**
❏ **Physical Examination**
❏ **Fluid Checks**
       ❏ **Lead Screening**
       ❏ **Tuberculin Test**
❏ **Immunizations**
       ❏ **Hepatitis B (HepB) – fourth dose**
       ❏ **Haemophilus Influenzae, Type b (Hib) – fourth dose**
       ❏ **Pneumococcal (PCV) – fourth dose**
       ❏ **Influenza – seasonal, yearly, various installation options available (consult with service provider)**
       ❏ **Measles, Mumps, Rubella (MMR) – first dose**
       ❏ **Varicella (VARICELLA) – first dose**
       ❏ **Hepatitis A (HepA) – first dose**
❏ **Oral Examination**
❏ **Notes** _____

Scheduled Maintenance Performed by _____

Frequently Asked Questions

Can my baby overheat?

Yes. When a baby overheats, the condition is referred to as fever. Fever is not in and of itself a major problem. It is a sign of an infection, and nearly every infection (most of which are viral) is accompanied by a temperature. Fever also plays a constructive role in slowing the spread of infections: viruses replicate less rapidly in a hot environment. Some service providers feel that fevers lower than 100°Fahrenheit (39.5°C) need not be treated.

The significance of a fever depends on how high it is, how long it has persisted, and other associated symptoms. A temperature of 103.5°F usually requires tepid, clean-sponge bathing, along with the administration of acetaminophen or ibuprofen. If your baby has had a temperature for more than three days, you should contact your service provider.

If your baby is lethargic or exhibits vomiting, a stiff neck, significant pain, respiratory distress (fast respiratory rate or the use of auxiliary muscles to breathe), or has a rash, you should also contact your service provider.

When should my baby start to eat solid foods?

From a nutritional and developmental standpoint, babies do not need to start solid foods until age six to nine months. A good cue that your child is ready is when she exhibits a curiosity about solid foods.

How many diapers will I use and when can I start toilet training my baby?

On average, a new baby will require 2,200 to 2,900 diaper changes in the first year of life alone! At what point you begin to toilet train your baby depends on cultural and lifestyle influences. Some users begin in the baby's first week, holding the baby over a potty when the first signs of a bowel movement are apparent. Many users begin toilet training sometime after eighteen months, when the baby is in better control of bowel function and able to communicate and appreciate a reward system. Still other users begin after the baby is three years old, when communication skills can speed the training process.

I update my baby's virus protection regularly, so why is he always sick?

During your baby's first year(s) of life, he will be developing an immune system. Even if your service provider performs regularly scheduled maintenance and updates, 70 percent of the illnesses affecting babies and young children are viral; these are generally cured and treated by a person's own immune system. When your baby is exposed to a new viral illness, the sickness is an opportunity for him to develop an immunity to it.

Generally, a baby will experience many sicknesses during the first year of life. More frequent illness may be an indication of allergies or may be more significant if your baby experiences recurrent serious bacterial infections, such as pneumonia, staphylococcal infections, and meningitis. In these cases, you should contact your service provider.

Are service providers available 24/7? Whom do I contact after hours?

In case of an emergency, always dial 911 first. If the after-hours situation appears not to be life-threatening but does require attention, most service providers have on-call access to them or another service provider in their medical group. Be sure to secure your service provider's answering service phone number and/or e-mail before the need arises. Some users, not wanting to disturb their service provider at all hours of the night or on weekends, may elect to use a freestanding medical facility. In such cases, be sure to update your service provider by phone, because reports of these incidents will not automatically be sent to her.

Should I really immunize my baby?

Currently, users asking this question tend to fall into one of three categories:

[1] Users who update their baby's virus software and immunize according to the CDC schedule.

[2] Users who adopt a different schedule, either taking a longer time to immunize their baby or eliminating specific vaccines that concern them.

[3] Users who do not immunize at all.

Some users are concerned about the preservatives and/or additives used in the preparation of a specific vaccine. Thiomersal (a mercury preservative) has been eliminated from almost all current vaccines. Small amounts of aluminum are used as an additive to increase the effectiveness of some vaccines.

Because your baby does not have an auto-update feature preinstalled, it is your responsibility to gather all the necessary information to make an informed decision about your baby's health.

There's so much information out there. What should I believe?

Many new users faced with the necessity of caring for a baby discover an overabundance of information. Use the following guidelines to sort through it:

[1] Trust your own instincts and intuition.
\
[2] Adopt the view that you are responsible for your baby and that you are in charge of the situation.

[3] Know that no *one* person is an expert on *every* baby. Look for information that suits your personality and childrearing style.

Trouble-Shooting Guide

If your baby is not operating at peak efficiency, use the following trouble-shooting guide to solve some common problems. Should any of these problems persist, contact your baby's service provider.

PROBLEM	POSSIBLE CAUSE	POSSIBLE TREATMENT
Baby emits unpleasant odor . . .	Gas	Turn on a fan to remove odor from room.
	Soiled diaper	Remove and reinstall diaper.
that is unbearable/ frequent	Diarrhea	Treat for diarrhea (see pp. 206–207).
and waste is:		
Black	Meconium	None. Meconium comes preinstalled in your baby and should pass in 1–2 weeks after delivery.
Seedy	Breast milk	None. "Seedlike" appearance of waste for breastfeeding babies is normal.
Green	Peas	Your baby's power supply will affect the color and consistency of waste output. This is normal.

PROBLEM	POSSIBLE CAUSE	POSSIBLE TREATMENT
Baby does not emit unpleasant odor.	Constipation	Your baby's power supply will affect the color and consistency of waste output. This is normal. Test baby's temperature at buttock port. Insert partial glycerine suppository. Contact service provider if waste is not produced.
Baby appears to be leaking from the . . .		
Optical sensors	Multiple	See "Baby cries" (pp. 246–247).
Nose	Allergic, teething, or sick	Wipe baby's nose with a soft tissue. Consult service provider.
Mouth	Teething	Offer frozen or cold chewable items. Cover baby's front with bib to absorb leakage from mouth port.
Waist	Tank is full	See "Expels ingested food" (p. 246).
	Improperly installed diaper	Remove and reinstall diaper, point penis downward (male models only).
	Diaper is overcapacity	Remove and reinstall diaper.

PROBLEM	POSSIBLE CAUSE	POSSIBLE TREATMENT
Baby does not appear to be leaking from waist.	Dehydration	Increase fluid/liquid intake of baby. Introduce Pediatric Electrolyte solution. Consult service provider.
Baby will not ingest food	Tank is full	Wait for 60 minutes and attempt to reinstall power supply.
	Sick	Consult service provider.
Expels ingested food	Tank is full	Stop feeding baby.
	Gassy	Burp baby. Wipe expelled food from clothing.
	Sick	Consult service provider.
Baby cries when placed: Vertically	Wet or soiled diaper	Remove and reinstall fresh diaper.
	Hungry	Feed baby.
	Hot	Observe and change baby's clothing and coverings.
	Cold	Observe and change baby's clothing and coverings.
	Tired	Activate SLEEP MODE.
	Gassy	Burp the baby.
	Lonely, scared, injured	Love and/or comfort the baby. Install pacification tool, natural or artificial.

PROBLEM	POSSIBLE CAUSE	POSSIBLE TREATMENT
Baby cries when placed:		
Horizontally	Ear infection	Place 1 small drop of warm olive oil in each of baby's auditory sensors.
In any position	Sick, teething, colicky	If crying persists for more than 30 minutes, consult service provider.
Baby will not . . .		
Enter SLEEP MODE	Not tired	Play with baby. Take baby for walk.
Reenter SLEEP MODE	Overtired/ overstimulated	Stop stimulating baby. Turn off lights. Rock baby gently. Attempt to reactivate SLEEP MODE.
Remain in SLEEP MODE	Wet or soiled diaper	Remove and reinstall diaper.
	Hungry	Feed baby.
	Uncomfortable	Check to be sure no tags or toys are poking baby. Change baby's clothes. Remove or add a light sheet or blanket.

PROBLEM	POSSIBLE CAUSE	POSSIBLE TREATMENT
Baby will not . . . Enter, reenter, or remain in SLEEP MODE no matter what I do.	Scared Does not know how	Love and comfort baby. Teach baby to Self- or User-Activate SLEEP MODE. Good luck. This too shall pass.

Index

About the Authors

A board-certified pediatrician with the American Academy of Pediatrics, DR. LOUIS BORGENICHT has run his own practice in Salt Lake City for the last 16 years. He is also Assistant Professor of Pediatrics at The University of Utah School of Medicine, and he serves on the Board of Directors for Physicians for Social Responsibility. In 2002, *Ladies' Home Journal* named him the Best Pediatrician in Utah. Dr. Borgenicht lives with his wife, Jody, who has finally learned how to sleep through the night while her husband goes out on calls.

JOE BORGENICHT is a D.A.D. who frequently telephones his father for advice. He is also a writer, entrepreneur (www.rulegolf.com), and the co-author of *The Action Hero's Handbook*, *The Action Heroine's Handbook*, and *Undercover Golf*. He lives in Salt Lake City with his wife, Melanie, and their sons, Jonah and Eli (who still operate at peak efficiency after nearly a decade).

About the Illustrators

PAUL KEPPLE and JUDE BUFFUM are better known as the Philadelphia-based studio HEADCASE DESIGN, whose work has been featured in many design publications, such as *American Illustration, Communication Arts*, and *Print*. Paul worked at Running Press Book Publishers for several years before opening Headcase in 1998. Both graduated from the Tyler School of Art, where they now teach. When Jude was an infant, his owners would often program him for extended periods of sleep mode. Paul's owners, on the other hand, tried numerous times to return their model, believing his inability to grow hair was a manufacturer's defect.

OWNER'S CERTIFICATE

Congratulations! Now that you've studied all the instructions in this manual, you are fully prepared to maintain your new baby. With the proper care and attention, your model will provide you with a lifetime of fun and happiness. Enjoy!

Owner's name

Model's name

Model's date of delivery

Model's weight at birth

Model's length at birth

Model's gender

Model's eye color

Model's hair color

Need Technical Support? Download the Baby Owner's Data Tracker!

Created to complement *The Baby Owner's Manual*, this handy free app from Quirk Books provides indispensable tools for your baby's care and development during that special first year of life.

- Record your baby's weight and length and compare it to average percentiles.
- Track feeding and sleeping schedules.
- View essential data in visually captivating charts.
- Share your data via e-mail, photos, Facebook, and Twitter.
- And much more!

With its everyday usefulness and intuitive interface, the Baby Owner's Data Tracker app offers a personalized experience that you won't find anywhere else!

Available through the iTunes App Store or quirkbooks.com/babyownersmanual.